BRITAIN'S HISTORY
FROM THE AIR

QUEEN ELIZABETH I in Parliament. Members of the Lords are seated and the Commons are standing.

BRITAIN'S HISTORY
FROM THE AIR

PHOTOGRAPHS BY JASON HAWKES

TEXT BY JANE STRUTHERS

EBURY PRESS

LONDON

First published 1994

1 3 5 7 9 10 8 6 4 2

Photographs Copyright © 1994 Aerial Images Ltd

Designed by David Fordham

Picture research by Mary-Jane Gibson

First published in the United Kingdom in 1994 by
Ebury Press Limited
Random House, 20 Vauxhall Bridge Road, London SW1V 2SA

Random House Australia (Pty) Limited
20 Alfred Street, Milsons Point, Sydney,
New South Wales 2061, Australia

Random House New Zealand Limited
18 Poland Road, Glenfield
Auckland 10, New Zealand

Random House South Africa (Pty) Limited
Endulini, 5A Jubilee Road,
Parktown 2193, South Africa

Random House Group Limited Reg. No. 954009
www.randomhouse.co.uk

A CIP catalogue record for this book
is available from the British Library

Typeset by SX Composing, Rayleigh, Essex
Printed in Italy by New Interlitho

CONTENTS

A map of Britain indicating the places illustrated in the book.

London (inset)

- Regent's Park
- Whitehall Palace
- Buckingham Palace
- St Paul's Cathedral
- Kensington Palace
- Tower of London
- Royal Albert Hall
- Palace of Westminster
- Victoria & Albert Museum
- Syon House
- Greenwich Palace & Park
- Kew Gardens
- Westminster Abbey
- R. Thames
- Eltham Palace
- Richmond upon Thames
- Hampton Court

Main map

- HIGHLAND
- Culloden
- GRAMPIAN
- Balmoral
- Braemar Castle
- Glencoe
- Glamis Castle
- TAYSIDE
- Iona
- Scone Palace
- Huntingtower Castle
- St Andrews
- Lochleven Castle
- Falkland Palace
- CENTRAL
- FIFE
- Stirling Castle
- Dunfermline Abbey
- Bannockburn
- Linlithgow Palace
- Edinburgh Castle
- STRATHCLYDE
- LOTHIAN Palace of Holyroodhouse
- BORDERS
- Bamburgh Castle
- Dunstanburgh Castle
- DUMFRIES & GALLOWAY
- NORTHUMBERLAND
- TYNE & WEAR
- DURHAM
- CLEVELAND
- CUMBRIA
- NORTH YORKS
- HUMBERSIDE
- LANCS
- W. YORKS
- GREATER MANCHESTER
- S. YORKS
- Conwy Castle
- CHESHIRE
- DERBY
- LINCOLN
- Caernarfon Castle
- CLWYD
- NOTTS
- GWYNEDD
- Harlech Castle
- STAFFORD
- Sandringham House
- Castle Rising
- SHROPSHIRE
- LEICESTER
- Burghley House
- NORFOLK
- MIDLANDS
- CAMBRIDGE
- Kimbolton Castle
- POWYS
- WARWICK
- NORTHANTS
- DYFED
- HEREFORD & WORCESTER
- Charlecote Park
- Cambridge
- SUFFOLK
- Carreg Cennan Castle
- BEDS
- Blenheim Palace
- Hatfield House
- GLOS.
- Berkeley Castle
- Cirencester Park
- BUCKS
- ESSEX
- Oxford
- HERTS
- Epping Forest
- GWENT
- OXFORD
- Highgrove Hse
- Henley-on-Thames
- LONDON
- W. MID. GLAMORGAN S.
- AVON
- WILTS
- Windsor Castle
- BERKS
- Ascot Racecourse
- Knole
- Canterbury Cathedral
- Longleat House
- Polesden Lacey
- SURREY
- Leeds Castle
- Dover Castle
- Glastonbury Tor
- Winchester Cath.
- Hever Castle
- KENT
- SOMERSET
- HANTS
- WEST SUSSEX
- Lewes
- E. SUSSEX
- Battle Abbey
- Tintagel Castle
- DEVON
- The New Forest
- DORSET
- Goodwood House
- Arundel Castle
- Brighton Pavilion
- Pevensey Castle
- Bodmin Moor
- Bosham
- Bognor Regis
- Carisbrooke Castle
- Osborne House
- St Michael's Mount
- CORNWALL
- ISLE of WIGHT

INTRODUCTION

The art of Biography
Is different from Geography.
Geography is about maps,
But Biography is about chaps.

THESE WORDS OF E. C. BENTLEY kept going through my head while I wrote this book, except that mentally I changed the word biography to history. That's because the more I researched the places that are included in the book, the more I realized that history – and especially royal history – is all about people and the stories that surrounded them. They are what I have put into this book – the stories, snippets of gossip and, in some cases, frankly odd tales about members of British royalty through the ages.

Some kings and queens came vividly to life as I read about them, although I must admit it was usually their misdeeds rather than their good ones that captured my imagination. In our present climate of prince-baiting and queen-bashing, it was fascinating to discover that nothing changes. The queen of Edward II was openly known during her lifetime as Isabella the She-Wolf of France, and after Queen Victoria was widowed and became friendly with her Scots servant John Brown, she was referred to as Mrs Brown by members of society. In fact, some kings and queens from Britain's past were so interesting and cropped up so often in the stories associated with the places in this book that sometimes I had to make a conscious effort to ignore them and write of less colourful people instead. If I hadn't done so, people like Henry VIII (whose life was such a fascinating combination of piety, duty and delusion), and George IV (who attended his own coronation in full make-up which then ran during the ceremony because it was such a hot July day) would have taken over completely.

Royal Britain from the Air is the third in this highly acclaimed series of books with aerial photography by Jason Hawkes. Once again he has worked his magic to create stunning photographs and often unusual viewpoints of some very well-known places. For the information of photography enthusiasts, Jason used a Pentax 645 with an inbuilt light meter, 150mm and 45mm lenses with an 80-160 zoom, and used Kodak 220 EPN. His partner in Aerial Images, Tim Kendall, navigated and assisted Jason on board the hired helicopter, and also edited the final choice of transparencies.

The map shows which places in Britain have been included in this book, but I must point out that the very nature of the subject matter means that some aerial photographs of royal places cannot be included for security reasons. Nevertheless, there is plenty to choose from here, whether you are interested in castles, palaces, fortresses, churches, cathedrals, battlefields or legends. There are also contemporary illustrations and photographs of the kings and queens themselves, to further bring to life the sometimes incredible stories that are associated with Britain's long tradition of royalty and which range from murder, divorce and intrigue to political alliances, failed ambitions and the one magic ingredient, love. To coin a phrase, all human life is here.

Finally, I should like to thank Mary Scott and Julian Shuckburgh of Ebury Press for all their help and support, David Fordham for designing another lovely book and William Martin for his unfailing support and enthusiasm.

Jane Struthers, London 1994

To Rosemary Kendall

ALL THAT REMAINS of the 14th-century St Michael's Chapel is the tower standing like a lone sentinel on the top of Glastonbury Tor, yet people travel far and wide to make private pilgrimages to this spot where King Arthur is said to have come to die.

In Arthurian legend, the King was mortally wounded by his nephew Modred at the Battle of Camlann and carried by weeping maidens on a barge to the Isle of Avalon. What happened after that is not recorded, but it is widely believed that Glastonbury Tor is the Isle of Avalon. During the Dark Ages, when Arthur lived, most of Somerset was marshland and the Tor was cut off by sheets of water during floods and very high tides. In fact, the pagan Celts called it Ynys-witrin, the Island of Glass, and regarded it as a sacred site, as they did all islands. It is easy to imagine a wounded king landing on Glastonbury Tor, and this belief was bolstered in the 12th century when the bones of a tall man and a woman with yellow hair were discovered by the monks of St Michael's Chapel. It was claimed that a lead cross was also found in the grave, inscribed 'Here in the Isle of Avalon the famous King Arthur lies buried.' Of course, it might have been a genuine find, but scholars agree that it comes from a later time than Arthur's although it was apparently too old to be a 12th-century fake. Sir Thomas Malory, who was one of the many medieval writers to be fascinated by the story of King Arthur and wrote his own romantic version of it, had a different inscription for Arthur's grave. According to him, it reads 'Here lies Arthur, the Once and Future King' – in other words, the King who will rise again whenever he is needed.

DID KING ARTHUR EXIST, or is he just the subject of a Celtic legend that has gathered momentum down the centuries, fuelled by poems, books, films and archaeological excavations that neither prove nor disprove his existence? Perhaps the answer is that, as with the Loch Ness Monster and Father Christmas, you should believe what you want to believe.

According to legend, which describes virtually every story that concerns King Arthur, he was born at a fortress here, son of the King Uther Pendragon. With the help of some magic from his assistant Merlin, Pendragon entered the castle disguised as the husband of the beautiful Igerna, wife of the Earl of Cornwall, and seduced her. The young King Arthur was born nine months later. Recent excavations have revealed that a monastery did stand here at around the time that Arthur would have lived (some time during the 6th century), although it is unlikely that Arthur would have been born there. It does not help that his possible life took place during the Dark Ages, so-called because there is so little documentary evidence about them. However, it is increasingly being accepted that a king, or certainly a leader, called Arthur did live during the 5th or 6th century and led a successful Celtic rally against the invading Anglo-Saxons.

Geoffrey of Monmouth, writing his *History of the Kings of Britain* in the 1130s, was the first great chronicler of Arthur's story, although other writers such as Dryden, Malory and Tennyson have followed suit. Twenty years later, the poet Robert Wace took Geoffrey's mixture of fact and fiction and added his own touches, which included the famous Round Table. As other writers joined in, the stories surrounding Arthur continued to depart from the original facts and introduced such new items as the love between Lancelot and Guinevere, and Galahad and his quest for the Holy Grail.

Even real kings themselves, beginning with the Plantagenets, were fascinated by the story of this legendary man who was mortally wounded in battle and was borne away to the mysterious Isle of Avalon, where his wounds were tended. But they did not care for the second half of the story, the one which said that he is sleeping until his people need him, when he will return. That allowed far too much room for trouble, because what would they do if someone appeared claiming to be Arthur? So Henry II announced that Arthur had died and been buried at Glastonbury, which was another name for Avalon. In 1191 Richard I apparently gave Arthur's sword, Excalibur, to Tancred, King of Sicily, which effectively scotched that part of the story. Monks at Glastonbury claimed that they had found a coffin made from a hollow log and that it contained Arthur's bones. In the same grave was a woman's skeleton with yellow hair, and they said she was Guinevere, Arthur's queen. Edward I was present at Glastonbury Abbey when the bones were given a ceremonial reburial. Edward III founded his Order of the Garter in an attempt to recreate the loyalty and solidarity enjoyed by the Knights of Arthur's Round Table and James I of England had his ancestry traced back to Arthur, in an attempt to prove his worthiness to rule both England and Scotland.

But what of the castle itself? Whether or not King Arthur lived, Tintagel has plenty of links with royalty. It also has a most intriguing setting, being built partly on the mainland and partly on a rocky island with a causeway linking the two. The earliest parts of the castle that stands today were built in about 1145 by Reginald, Earl of Cornwall. Considerable building work was carried out by Earl Richard, the younger brother of Henry III, between 1236 and 1272. In due course ownership of the building passed to the romantically named Black Prince, but it was at this point that the castle began to show signs of dilapidation. Matters went from bad to worse, with an ignominious period when it served as a prison, and today little of the castle remains. Nevertheless, that has not deterred generations of believers in King Arthur from coming here and tramping up the many steps that lead to the summit of The Island. Nearby is Merlin's Cave, where the young Arthur is said to have met the eponymous wizard. The supposed connections with King Arthur have given Tintagel a thriving local industry, as well as an atmosphere and mystery that show no signs of abating.

A ROYAL VISIT to Cornwall: the Prince and Princess of Wales (later King Edward VI and Queen Alexandra) land at St Michael's Mount.

THE IMAGINATION of even the most hard-nosed visitor is caught by the sight of St Michael's Mount out in the waters off the south coast of Cornwall. It is dedicated to the Archangel, who is said to have appeared to local fishermen in AD 495.

St Michael's Mount is the twin of Mont St Michel in Normandy and was built by its Abbot in 1135. It remained attached to its French namesake for almost 350 years, after which time it changed hands and was owned by a convent in Syon. St Michael's Mount suffered during the Dissolution of the Monasteries by Henry VIII and was turned into a fortress, and frequently acted as a garrison during the Civil War. The St Aubyn family acquired it in 1657 and have lived here more or less ever since, although it is now owned by the National Trust.

St Michael's Mount has another claim to fame, because it is said to belong to part of the lost land of Lyonesse, a legendary kingdom that apparently stretched from Cornwall to the Scilly Isles. All that remains of this land, which was ruled over by the semi-legendary King Arthur, are the Scilly Isles themselves. Interestingly enough, the Cornish name for St Michael's Mount is *Carrick luz en cuz*, which meands 'the ancient rock in the wood', and at low tide the fossilized remains of a forest which once covered the whole of this stretch of coast can be seen. Perhaps the lost kingdom of Lyonesse is not just a legend after all?

CHARLES I gazes forlornly through the barred window of his prison at Carisbrooke Castle in 1648. His exhortation to 'Behold your King' ultimately fell on stony ground.

IN THE DAYS when there was a Lord of the Isle of Wight, he lived on the island at Carisbrooke Castle, so it was the local seat of government. There was once a Roman villa on the site, but the keep and curtain wall of the present castle were completed in 1136, with the domestic buildings added in the following century. The huge gatehouse, with its drum towers, dominates the castle, but was not considered imposing enough during the Spanish Armada, so Elizabeth I ordered that the castle should be refortified and strengthened.

In the event the castle was not attacked, but it was not the first time that it had been placed under threat. Carisbrooke had been garrisoned in 1136 and was unsuccessfully attacked by the French during the reign of Richard II. However, its most notable royal association is with the doomed Charles I, who fled from the Parliamentarian army at Hampton Court to the Isle of Wight in November 1647. He was in fear of his life and afraid that the army at Hampton Court would assassinate him, but in the event he simply swapped one place of imprisonment for another. Carisbrooke Castle became his new prison, and he stayed here for fourteen months. At first he was able to enjoy comparative freedom, but once news leaked out of his secret negotiations with the Scots in which he would be restored to their throne, his life at Carisbrooke became much harder. Nevertheless, he was determined to escape and might have done so in 1648 had he not got wedged between the bars of his bedroom window in the attempt. When he finally left Carisbrooke it was not of his own volition – he was sent back to London, to stand trial (whose outcome was a foregone conclusion) and face his subsequent execution. The church of St Nicholas, which stands in the grounds of the castle, was rebuilt and opened in 1904 in memory of Charles I.

Carisbrooke had another royal inhabitant in the late 19th century when Princess Beatrice, the youngest daughter of Queen Victoria, lived here with her husband, who was governor of the island. When he died in 1896 she took over the position. Another illustrious governor was the late Earl Mountbatten of Burma, who was made governor in 1965 by Elizabeth II. Today, the castle is open to visitors.

THE JAGGED RUINS of Pevensey Castle are a rather sad reminder of what was once an important medieval fortress, but then little is as it was on this marshy stretch of the Sussex coast. For when Pevensey Castle was built, sea water surrounded it on three sides. Today, the rapidly changing landscape of the past millennium means the castle stands about 1 mile inland. Nor is this the first castle to have been built here – the present-day castle is enclosed within the walls of the Roman fortress Anderida, which was built at the end of the 3rd century to repel Saxon invaders.

The Norman castle was built for the same defensive purpose although, like Anderida, it was constructed by invaders rather than the defending countrymen. It marks the place where William the Conqueror and his band of Norman soldiers landed at Pevensey on 28 September 1066 at the start of the Norman invasion. William had arrived to fight King Harold for his crown and the right to rule England and Wales. He reasoned that Pevensey was a vulnerable place, and so commanded his half-brother, Robert of Mortain, to build a castle on that particular piece of coastline to deter anyone who wanted to follow in his footsteps. By this time, his conquest had been successful, having fought and killed King Harold at the Battle of Hastings on 14 October 1066. So as to drive his point home, William ordered that Harold's slain body should be buried on the Pevensey seashore. Given the way this piece of coastline has filled out so much since the 11th century, Harold's ignominious burial place is now somewhere

under Pevensey High Street – or would be, if his corpse had not been dug up and given formal burial at Waltham Abbey in Essex, which he founded in 1060.

As well as Pevensey, William I quickly had a chain of other defensive castles and fortresses constructed in Sussex, including the once mighty Hastings Castle which stood high on the cliffs looking out across the English Channel at Hastings. It was ruined during a violent storm in 1287 when the sea washed most of it away.

The sea also spelt ruin for Pevensey, because as it slowly retreated southwards and the land filled in, the castle became marooned on the flat marshland that is now called the Pevensey Levels. Nevertheless, the Norman invasion was not the only time that Pevensey played a part in British history. During the Napoleonic Wars of the early 19th century, a string of Martello towers was built along the South Coast, stretching from Seaford in Sussex to Aldeburgh in Suffolk, fortified to repel the expected French invasion. Martello towers, looking like huge upturned buckets, stand guard either side of Pevensey Bay (as the village on the present-day seashore is called). They were never used, because Napoleon eventually changed his mind about invading Britain. Pevensey Castle, however, was used again as a fortress during the Second World War, when the towers were renovated and pillboxes were built on the keep. They can still be seen and visited today, as can the outlying walls of the castle which were built by the Romans so long ago.

THE SCOTTISH SEASIDE TOWN of St Andrews grew up around the 12th-century cathedral, although only its ruins are still standing today. Work began on it in 1160 but it was not consecrated until 1318, when Robert the Bruce gave thanks for his victory against Edward II's English army at Bannockburn four years earlier. The university was built here in 1450 by Bishop Kennedy, one of the Regents of the young James II of Scotland, and was the first to be founded in Scotland.

In June 1538, Mary of Guise married James V in the cathedral following a marriage that had already taken place by proxy. Mary was anxious to marry James because the widowed Henry VIII had been considering whether to make her wife number four. As his marital track record was hardly encouraging to a prospective bride she wanted to ensure that she was unavailable, so brought forward her wedding, which had already been contracted. Mary Queen of Scots, the daughter of Mary and James, visited St Andrews several times, staying in what is now called Queen Mary's House.

SET IN THE LOMOND HILLS in Fife, Falkland Palace has everything that a good castle needs. It's got plenty of history, important royal associations and a tremendous amount of atmosphere, which was thoughtfully provided by a case of imprisonment and subsequent murder.

The palace that stands today is the second to have been built on this site, and it was constructed at the beginning of the 16th century to replace the much earlier building. This was originally the hunting tower belonging to the Macduffs, who were the Earls of Fife, but ownership of the tower was transferred, with the earldom, to Robert Stewart in 1371. He was the second son of King Robert II, founder of the Stuart dynasty, but like so many younger princes of the time, he had his eye firmly fixed on the throne. Robert III, his brother, had been crippled by a blow from a horse, so a battle for the power behind the throne began between Robert Stewart and his nephew, David, Duke of Rothesay. In 1402 David was taken to Falkland by force and left there to starve to death. Robert Stewart never got the power he sought because in due course the crown passed to Robert III's second son, who became James I of Scotland.

When the new palace was built it was in the style of the Scottish Gothic, but the improvements carried out by James V between 1537 and 1542 turned the palace into a *château*. James died here on 14 December 1542 and his week-old daughter, Mary Queen of Scots, became Queen. Her reign was largely difficult and deeply troubled, but between 1561 and 1565 she spent happy times here hunting in the hills, before losing her throne in 1567.

ALTHOUGH IT NOW LIES INLAND, Castle Rising was originally a port on The Wash, in a stretch of coastline thronged with villages and towns whose names testify to their ancient associations with the sea. Today it is dominated by the Norman castle built by William de Albini, who became Earl of Lincoln after marrying Adela, the widow of Henry I. The massive walls of the castle – up to 9 ft thick in some places in the keep – were built for defensive reasons.

For nearly thirty years, the most notorious inhabitant of Castle Rising was the 'She-wolf', as Queen Isabella, the scheming wife of Edward II, was called. She was banished here by her son, Edward III, after she and her lover had conspired to murder her husband and take the throne for themselves.

Isabella, the daughter of Philip IV the Fair of France and Joan of Champagne, married the weak and ineffectual Edward II in 1308. Although it united the thrones of England and France it was not a marriage made in heaven, and Isabella was deeply annoyed, to say the least, when her new husband lavished all her most beautiful and expensive wedding presents on his friend and favourite, Piers Gaveston. At his coronation, Edward even went so far as to say he preferred Gaveston's couch to that of his new wife. Gaveston was a Gascon knight who had been banished from England by Edward's father, Edward I, and he was eventually beheaded in 1312, the same year in which Edward III, Edward and Isabella's first child, was born.

Isabella liked to keep a controlling interest in both the English and French thrones. Not only did she intercede in a dispute between her husband and some English barons, who were trying to limit royal power, but she was also at the centre of a plot to accuse her two French sisters-in-law of adultery, probably in the hope that the legitimacy of their children would be put in doubt and the French throne would pass to her son, the future Edward III.

That plot failed and Isabella began to cast covetous eyes on the English throne. Edward, never an effective or impressive king, had by now handed over virtually all his power to the baron Hugh le Despenser and his son, and although they originally ran the country sensibly they soon became greedy for more power and more money. When they reduced Isabella's retinue (originally 180-strong) and put her on a small daily allowance, she was determined to wreak her revenge. During a diplomatic mission to France she joined forces with Roger Mortimer, a baron who had been exiled from England, and announced she would not return to England while the Despensers remained Edward's favourites. She and Mortimer duly landed at Orwell in Essex in September 1326, determined to take the crown for themselves, and pursued Edward to the young Despenser's estates in Glamorgan, where he was eventually captured. Isabella had both Despensers murdered, and imprisoned Edward at Kenilworth Castle.

In January 1327 Edward was forced to abdicate and the young Prince Edward was crowned Edward III of England on 29 January 1327, but there was no question of the fifteen-year-old boy ruling the country. Isabella wanted that privilege for herself, and for the next four years she and Mortimer enjoyed just that. In the meantime, because their joint rulership was so shaky and Edward II's continued existence a source of potential trouble, they had to do away with him, and he was eventually murdered in September 1327.

Finally, in 1330, Edward III staged a coup against his mother and her lover. He had Mortimer executed and sent Isabella off to Castle Rising, with an annual allowance of £3000. She lived there until her death in 1358. In a final, curious twist to the story, her body was buried in London but her heart was taken to Gloucester Abbey, to join the body of her husband whose brutal murder she had arranged thirty years before.

The roof and floors of the castle have long since crumbled away but what remains is very impressive and imposing. It is easy to imagine the savage Isabella living here, especially as the castle is set amid some large Norman earthworks which add to the atmosphere of the place. There are also a ruined Norman church and gatehouse, both of which were built before the squat keep. The size of the rooms in the keep testify to the importance of Castle Rising when it was built. It must have been a fitting prison for a queen.

EDWARD II abdicated at Kenilworth Castle on 20 January 1327. He is shown here handing over the sceptre and orb to Sir William Trussell and other deputies.

THE STORY OF EDWARD II'S IMPRISONMENT and subsequent death at Berkeley Castle in Gloucestershire is a grisly one, full of the stuff of medieval cruelty and involving a weak king, a power-hungry wife and a chase across the south of England from Essex to Glamorgan, where the King was finally captured.

Edward II had long since incurred the displeasure of his wife and the country as he mismanaged many affairs of State, was more interested in enjoying himself than ruling England, and continually surrounded himself with scheming favourites – first Piers Gaveston and later the hated Despensers. Yet even though he had skirmishes with barons, he was to discover that his greatest enemy of all was his Queen, Isabella.

When war broke out between England and France over Gascony, Isabella was the obvious person to send on a diplomatic mission, as the French king was her brother, Charles IV. However, what Edward had not foreseen was that, while in Paris, Isabella would join forces with one of Edward's disaffected barons, Roger Mortimer, and plot to overthrow the English throne. She and Mortimer landed on English soil in September 1326 and eventually captured the fugitive Edward in Wales. He was taken to Kenilworth Castle and forced to abdicate in January 1327. His son, Edward III, was crowned in the same month, but not allowed to reign. His mother and Mortimer did that for him.

But what could they do about Edward II? It was far too dangerous to leave him languishing at Kenilworth alive, so Berkeley Castle was chosen as his final destination. Two of Isabella's agents, Maltravers and Gournay, took the castle from Thomas Berkeley, whose family had owned it since 1086, and sent Edward there in April 1327. Thomas Berkeley, who was a kind man and had nothing to do with Edward's imprisonment or subsequent death, was told to absent himself and so went to live at another of his estates. Maltravers and Gournay hoped that if they treated Edward badly enough he would die of natural causes, so they hollowed out a cellar below his cell and filled it with rotting corpses. They hoped that the putrid air would finish him off, but his strong constitution miraculously survived such a hideous fate. However, the final indignity imposed on him was much worse. On 21 September 1327 Edward was disembowelled with a red hot poker, although his murderers took great care to ensure that no burn marks were found on his body. It was announced that he had died of natural causes, and he was buried in St Peter's Abbey at Gloucester, which is now Gloucester Cathedral.

Anyone with a taste for the morbid and grisly will enter Berkeley Castle today and march straight over to the grille cut in the wall of the King's Gallery, then peer down into the small dungeon (now known as King Edward's Room) in which the sorry king lived out his last miserable months. Mercifully there is no longer any suggestion of the hideous smells he was forced to live with, but it would surely be unnerving to be in that small room at dusk. The rest of the castle is cheerful and beautiful, although the huge skewers and spits hanging up in the kitchen bear an uncomfortable resemblance to medieval instruments of torture.

The exterior of the castle is quite stunning, and serves as a reminder that the castle was originally built as a fortress. In fact, the meadows that stretch away in all directions could once be flooded whenever necessary, in order to keep out any unwelcome visitors. The pink and grey stone of the walls can look ethereal in certain lights and are a sight matched in eeriness by the sound of the nearby Berkshire Hunt tearing across the fields, with bugles blowing and beagles barking.

AFTER FLEEING FOR HIS LIFE to France in 1651, the exiled Charles II did not set foot on British soil again until 25 May 1660, when he landed at Dover. The young Samuel Pepys was with him.

IT WAS HENRY II who built the first stone castle to stand on this site, although the earthworks around it date back much earlier than the 12th century of Henry's rule. Henry knew it was essential to build a massive fortification here because he needed to guard the English Channel from the French and other enemies, and as Dover marked the narrowest point of the Channel it was important to ensure that the castle would be as impregnable as it was possible to make it. Henry built a wall around the Norman moat and added a keep, and the building of the surrounding fortifications was continued by his son Richard I (more romantically known as Richard Coeur de Lion) and later, after Richard's death, by Henry's other son, King John. John was less romantically known as Lackland, because his father did not leave him any major Continental lands in his will.

It was during John's unhappy reign that Dover's vulnerability was discovered. In 1216 the castle was besieged by Prince Louis of France, who was eager to take the English throne and was being actively encouraged to do so by the disaffected English barons. Dover's eastern tower collapsed. It was during his campaign against Louis that John lost most of his baggage train in The Wash, and he died soon after, in October 1216, at Newark. Most of the support for Louis had had more to do with hatred for John than enthusiasm for Louis, and with John's death his popularity began to decline. He departed for France to muster more support but when he returned his forces were defeated at Lincoln. A French fleet sent to relieve Louis was involved in a battle in August 1217 and Louis was finally bought off the following month, accepting 10,000 marks to relinquish his claims to the English throne.

When Henry III succeeded to the throne after the death of his father, John, he ensured that Dover Castle was strengthened again, and by 1256 the castle would never be so strong, nor so large, again. It had at least seventeen towers, and today the castle (which is open to the public) looks much as it did in Henry III's reign, despite having the tops of many of its towers chopped off during the Napoleonic Wars to provide artillery platforms in the event of the expected French invasion, which never came.

Until the viking raiders overran the north-east of Britain in the 9th century, Bamburgh was one of the principal strongholds of the Anglo-Saxon kings of Northumbria. This kingdom was created after AD 600, when Bernicia (mostly Northumberland) and Deira (mostly Humberside) were joined together, and eventually covered all land south of the Firth of Forth and north of the Mersey and Humber. It was part of the so-called Heptarchy – the seven major Anglo-Saxon kingdoms of Kent, Essex, East Anglia, Sussex, Mercia, Wessex and Northumbria.

The Saxon king Ida captured Bamburgh, which was then part of Bernicia, in 547, and although Northumbria had passed its military peak by 685 it was nevertheless a renowned area for scholarship and learning. King Oswald I of Northumbria, who ruled in the 7th century, made Bamburgh the capital of his kingdom but in 866-7 the Danish Great Army arrived and pillaged their way through Northumbria.

The castle that stands today was built in the 12th century, as the previous Saxon fortification was besieged by William II at the end of the 11th century. The new Norman castle, which was built during the following hundred years, was virtually complete by the time Henry II built the double-towered east gate and other major additions. The castle was the focus of several sieges, and during the Wars of the Roses was retained by the Lancastrian supporters of Margaret of Anjou (the wife of the deposed Henry VI) in 1461 after Edward IV had seized the English throne. It was one of several bases that allowed the Lancastrians to control most of Northumberland, but was besieged by Edward in December 1462 and finally surrendered, under gunfire, in 1463. After that it fell into rack and ruin and was only restored by the 1st Lord Armstrong, the arms manufacturer, in the 1890s. The interior of the castle is a fine example of Victorian medieval fantasy, and the Great Hall has a hammerbeam roof made from solid teak. Arms and armour are on display and, for the less military minded, there are also fine collections of porcelain, Fabergé *objets d'art* and tapestries.

ON A HEADLAND immediately north of the river Tyne, once known as Penbal Crag, a Christian monastery has existed since at least the seventh century, and was once famous for being the burial place of St Oswin, the murdered King of Deira. Heribald, a friend of the Venerable Bede who died in 735, was abbot for a time. This building did not survive the Danish invasions, being eventually destroyed in 875; but after the Norman conquest the present Benedictine priory was refounded, as a dependency of St Albans Abbey. But because of the exceptional defensive qualities of the site, and the insecurities of the border region in general throughout the Middle Ages, the priory was developed within a castle enclosure – of which now only the 14th-century gatehouse remains.

After the dissolution of the monasteries in 1539, the site became part of Henry VIII's scheme of national defence: new fortifications were built, cannon installed, and a garrison of fifty men quartered in the castle and priory buildings. Over the next 300 years this military role continued, right through to the 20th century, when in 1905 modern gun batteries were installed for the defence of Tynemouth, and remained operational and fully manned (after further rehabilitation in 1914) throughout the Second World War. The guns were only removed in 1956.

The grassy emptiness seen today is therefore misleading. In the Middle Ages the headland was full of buildings – monks' cloisters, accommodation for guests and pilgrims, and barns and farm buildings which provided the subsistence base for the priory. Later, there would have been soldiers' barracks, magazines and storage buildings. All we see today are the remains of the medieval priory and fortifications, the coastguard station and remains of the artillery platforms, and the burial ground containing some 700 gravestones – including a memorial to Corporal Alexander Rollo, who held the lantern at the burial of Sir John Moore at Corunna in 1809, during the Peninsular War.

MARY QUEEN OF SCOTS was imprisoned at Lochleven Castle between June 1567 and May 1568. She is shown here in the castle with her reduced retinue.

THE 14TH-CENTURY STATE PRISON of Lochleven, built on an island in the middle of Loch Leven, is one of the landmarks in the tragic story of Mary Queen of Scots. It was here that she was imprisoned for nearly a year, between June 1567 and her escape in May 1568.

Mary was sent here after the murder of Lord Darnley, her second husband. Her fortunes continued to go from bad to worse, with the Scots people turning against her just when she needed their support more than ever. For the Scots, the final straw had come when Mary had married the Earl of Bothwell, the man popularly suspected of being Darnley's murderer, only three months after her husband's death. What they did not realize was that Mary was forced into the marriage, because after she had refused Bothwell's first proposal he intercepted her journey from Edinburgh to Stirling, where her son (the future James VI of Scotland and James I of England) was, and told her there was talk of a rebellion against her. He suggested she follow him to the safety of Dunbar Castle, which she did, but once there he either raped or seduced her. Whatever happened, she was compromised and forced into marrying him, which she did on 15 May 1567 after Bothwell's divorce from his first wife. By all accounts it was a miserable marriage, even though it only lasted a month.

Public opinion was now one of outrage against Mary, and the threat of rebellion grew. In June she and Bothwell were besieged in the castle of Borthwick, south of Edinburgh, and raised a few hundred men in their support. They rode to Carberry Hill and waited for the confederate lords – including the ubiquitous Lord Ruthven – to arrive. When they did, there were discussions between the two sides but no fighting, with Mary saying that the lords had been in favour of her marrying Bothwell in the past and had even signed a bond saying so. While all this was going on, the royal troops began melting away and Bothwell said he would go to Dunbar to raise support. It was the last Mary ever saw of him, because although he tried to rally support he failed, and eventually had to escape to the Orkneys. Mary surrendered, believing that she would be treated well, but immediately the soldiers started calling her a whore, and as she was led back to Edinburgh she was horrified to hear people calling out that she should be drowned.

The following day Mary was taken to Lochleven and imprisoned in the castle, with Ruthven acting as one of her two jailers. The Douglas family, who owned the castle, were supporters of the confederate lords, so Mary could expect no support from them. In July, her misery was compounded, first by a miscarriage and then by having to abdicate in favour of her son. Her brother, the Earl of Moray, acted as Regent. As the months wore on, Mary's considerable charm began to work its spell on George Douglas, one of the sons of the family, and he was determined to help her escape. Finally, after several abortive attempts, she was rowed across the loch on 2 May 1568 by Willy Douglas, an orphaned cousin of the family, and was finally at liberty once more.

Today Lochleven is a ruin, standing roofless but proud amidst a belt of trees on Castle Island. Visitors to the 14th-century castle are ferried out across Loch Leven from the jetty at Kinross. The remains of the great hall and kitchen, which were both built in the 16th century, can be found in the courtyard.

BRAEMAR AND SEPTEMBER are synonymous to visitors to Scotland who want to be sure of 'doing the season', for this is when the Braemar Highland Games are staged. They take place in the grounds of Braemar Castle, and are considered by many to be an essential part of late summer in Scotland, perhaps mostly because they are presided over by the royal family. At this point in the year they are always holidaying nearby at Balmoral, and Braemar is the capital of Royal Deeside.

Braemar Castle itself also has a distinguished royal link, for an earlier version of the building is believed to have been the hunting lodge of Malcolm III or 'Canmore' (meaning chief), that great Scots king who founded the dynasty of Dunkeld and married Margaret of England (later St Margaret of Scotland). The castle that stands today, however, was only built in 1628 by the Earl of Mar, who wanted an operational base from which to fight his rivals, the Farquharsons. In the event the castle was burnt down by a Farquharson during the Jacobite

uprising of 1689 which followed the Glorious Revolution, when James II fled for his life and William of Orange was invited to assume the throne. More Jacobite uprisings followed, first in support of the Old Pretender (the putative James VII of Scotland) in 1715, and then the Young Pretender (his son, Bonnie Prince Charlie) in 1745. When work on a new castle began in 1748, it was built as an army post from which the rebellious Highlanders could be controlled. Such a purpose is self-evident from the fortress-like appearance of the castle. A garrison lived here until 1797, when it was considered safe to remove them and adopt the castle as a private residence. The Farquharsons moved in, and their descendants still live here today. They open the castle to the public each summer.

The interior of the castle is impressive, with barrel-vaulted ceilings and an underground prison. Among the treasures at Braemar is a piece of tartan reputed to have been worn by Bonnie Prince Charlie – a fitting reminder of the castle's vivid and rebellious past.

THE HUGE, FORMIDABLE BULK of Harlech Castle was intended by Edward I to be overwhelming proof that he would resist and overcome any insurrection by the Welsh. The thick stone walls and prominent position of the castle – sitting on top of a 200-ft tall rocky peak – sent out an unequivocal message. Harlech Castle was built above Tremadoc Bay between 1286 and 1290, with the intention that food would be brought to the castle inmates across the water. The landward side was considered to be where any threats of attack would come from, so it was protected by a massive ditch, a curtain wall and a huge four-towered gatehouse, which also contained the private accommodation.

Harlech withstood one siege by the Welsh but fell in 1404 when Owain Glyndwr, Wales's great hero and self-proclaimed Prince of Wales, mounted a fierce attack on the castle after already raiding south Wales and laying waste to much of north Wales. He held Harlech for four years, only surrendering in February 1409 when his wife and grandchildren were taken prisoners. The castle was again taken during the Wars of the Roses, when it was held under siege by the Lancastrian supporter, Dafydd ap Ieuan ap Einion. He was eventually starved out and surrendered to Edward IV, but the song 'Men of Harlech' was composed to celebrate his bravery. Harlech was the last castle to be held by the Royalists during the Civil War, proving that Edward I's impressive fortress had certainly lived up to expectations. It can still be visited today – and you don't have to scale the ramparts to do it.

A DEFEATED MARY QUEEN OF SCOTS is escorted into Edinburgh
by the confederate lords in June 1567.

EDINBURGH CASTLE is perched high above the city of Edinburgh on Castle Rock, part of an extinct volcano like the neighbouring Arthur's Seat which shelters Holyroodhouse. The castle that stands today was begun during the 11th-century reign of Malcolm III and his wife, Queen (St) Margaret, but an earlier castle had been built here in the 7th century by Edwin, King of Northumbria. Until 1124, when David I succeeded to the Scottish throne, Dunfermline was the capital of Scotland, but he passed a decree changing it to Edinburgh.

The oldest part of the castle, and the oldest building still in use in Edinburgh, is the tiny St Margaret's Chapel, built by the Queen in 1076. She died at Edinburgh Castle after hearing of the deaths of her husband and son at the Battle of Alnwick. Her body was smuggled down the west cliff and buried at Dunfermline Abbey, across the Firth of Forth. The chapel is a rare example of Scottish Romanesque architecture and narrowly escaped the fate of all the other parts of the castle which were known to Margaret. When Robert the Bruce captured the castle from the English in 1313 he had every building, except the chapel, razed to the ground. After the Reformation, the chapel was used as an ammunition store until this century, when it was restored to its proper use.

Many Scottish monarchs contributed to Edinburgh Castle, either by adding buildings or participating in historical events. James IV, the king who was so keen to boost the standing of the city and succeeded magnificently before dying in battle at Flodden in 1513, built the Great Hall early in the 16th century, and Mary Queen of Scots gave birth here to her son, the future James VI of Scotland and James I of England, on 19 June 1566. She chose the castle in preference to Holyroodhouse because it was a place of greater safety – Riccio's murder had

taken place before her very eyes at Holyroodhouse only three months previously. Even so, she was very keen to assert the legitimacy of her new-born son, publicly displaying the young Prince James to her husband, Lord Darnley, and saying 'My Lord, God has given you and me a son, begotten by none but you.' She added, in a dig about Riccio's murder, that the baby was 'so much your own son, that I fear it will be the worse for him hereafter'.

During the Civil War, the 'Honours of Scotland' – the Scottish Crown Jewels – were removed from their home in the Castle and hidden in a church on the Kincardine coast. They were returned to the castle after the Restoration, in 1662, and cannons were discharged to celebrate their safe return. However, they were subsequently locked away in a chest in the castle and their whereabouts forgotten for more than a hundred years. It was Sir Walter Scott who instigated the search for them and he was present in 1818 when royal permission was given to open the chest in which they were presumed to reside. Sure enough, there they were. The crown, which was remodelled on the orders of James V in 1540, was last worn by Elizabeth II in 1953 on her State visit to Edinburgh after her coronation.

The brooding presence of the castle perched high on Castle Rock can be felt from many areas of Edinburgh, but is especially impressive when viewed from below in Princes Street Gardens. The castle can be visited all year round, but it really comes into its own during the annual Edinburgh Festival at the end of August, when the city is full of festival-goers and the castle esplanade is home every night to the Edinburgh Tattoo. With the castle bathed in soft floodlights and the massed bands of pipers playing Scots tunes, the tattoo is an incredible spectacle and a most memorable experience.

JAMES V, KING OF SCOTLAND, taking refuge at Stirling Castle, having escaped from the Regent Douglas.

STIRLING CASTLE bears many similarities to Edinburgh Castle, not only because both stand on huge crags of basaltic rock but because both have played a major part in Scottish history. Earlier wooden castles were built on this spot but the stone castle that still stands today was built mostly in the early 15th century. It replaced the ruins which were all that remained after the tumultuous events of the previous century. Stirling Castle was besieged by Edward I in 1304, held by the English for ten years, regained by Sir William Wallace, recaptured by the English and given back to the Scots after their triumphant victory at nearby Bannockburn in 1314 and subsequent independence from the English. Robert the Bruce slighted (damaged) it so it would be of no further use to the English, but nevertheless they recaptured it for a while and it was only restored to Scots' hands in 1347.

As befits a castle with such an exciting history, Stirling continued to be the site of some extraordinary scenes. The Stuart kings loved it here, and transformed it from a fortress into a beautiful royal palace. James II lured the 8th Earl of Douglas – a real trouble-maker – here in 1452, murdered him and had his body thrown out of a window. James IV built the great palace block and James VI built the Chapel Royal for the christening of his son, Prince Henry, in 1594. Sadly, this son, whom the Scots hoped would become king, died at the age of eighteen and his brother, Charles I, succeeded to the throne, only to be beheaded in 1649.

Mary Queen of Scots was crowned in Stirling's old chapel, called Holy Rood, in 1543 and her son, James VI, was christened there. After 1603, when the English throne passed to James VI, he abandoned his plans for improving the castle still further and moved his court to England. Stirling's greatest period of excitement was over.

Visitors to Stirling today can recapture some of that excitement, however, if they use their imaginations. Those with a military inclination will be interested to know that the castle contains the museum of the Argyll and Sutherland Highlanders, and also that the great battle of Bannockburn was played out on the surrounding land. There is also a visitor's centre, equipped with a cinema, that relates Stirling's long and fascinating history.

THERE ARE FEW CASTLES more impressive than Conwy, which was precisely what Edward I intended when he constructed his formidable chain of fortresses, known as the 'iron ring', across North Wales. Usually they were just impregnable (or so he hoped) castles, but at Conwy he went one better. The whole town was built as a garrison, with magnificent town walls which still stand today. They stretch for nearly one mile and have twenty-two towers. Yet one of the most impressive aspects of Conwy Castle is that it was built in five short years, between 1283 and 1288. James of St George, Master of the Royal Works, supervised the building work, as he did Edward's other Welsh castles, including Beaumaris, Harlech and Caernarfon. The walls of the castle are up to 15 ft thick in some places – a precaution that proved its worth when the Welsh besieged Edward in the castle in 1294. The next skirmish between the Welsh and the English at Conwy took place in 1401 when the Welsh overran the castle while its garrison were all at church.

By the 17th century Conwy had fallen into ruin, and was sold very cheaply to Viscount Conway. Nevertheless its royal links continued. During the Civil War Conwy was a Royalist stronghold, but it was attacked and captured by the Parliamentarians in 1646. Its decline continued, but today it is open to the public and is of particular interest because of the two massive bridges which stand either side of it – Sir Thomas Telford's construction of 1826 and that built by George Stephenson in 1848.

PRINCE CHARLES' investiture, Caernarfon.

CAERNARFON is a landmark in the bloody, bitter history of Wales, because it represents the final indignity to be imposed on the defeated Welsh by the English monarch Edward I. His father, Henry III, had conferred on him many of his Welsh lands and Edward was determined to make his mark on them. He imposed English laws in the parts of Wales he owned – a rash beginning and one which made him extremely unpopular. He recognized that the Welsh prince, Llewelyn ab Gruffydd, held great power but swiftly became irritated when Llewelyn failed to pay homage to him and, in revenge, Edward invaded North Wales in 1277. He conducted his campaign like a siege, forcing Llewellyn to surrender through lack of supplies. He then lost no time in stripping Llewellyn of much of his power. The Welsh resentment at having to concede to English laws gave Llewelyn the chance to fight back between 1282 and 1283, but Edward was stronger and systematically reinforced his supremacy by building a chain of fortresses across Wales. Yet Caernarfon was intended to be the greatest of the castles, and was modelled by the architect James of St George on the 5th-century walls of Constantinople.

Edward I's fourth son, who was to become the ill-fated Edward II, was born here in 1284 and named Prince of Wales in 1301. This announcement acted as further incentive for Welsh hatred because here was a man who had killed their own Welsh-born princes before imposing an English-born Prince of Wales on them. Legend has it that the Prince was presented to the Welsh as soon as he was born, but this story owes more to myth than fact.

Other royal kings named their eldest sons Prince of Wales, but it was not until 1911 that the first royal investiture was held here, when the future Edward VIII was named Prince of Wales. In 1969 the investiture of Prince Charles took place and was televised. The Prince's uncle, the Earl of Snowdon, stage-managed the proceedings which, despite taking place beneath a very modern-looking glass canopy, had a magnificently medieval atmosphere. The Prince, wishing to appease any Welsh ill-feeling, had spent a term at Aberystwyth University learning the Welsh language. However, Welsh nationalists were not impressed and vented their feelings in a spate of bombings, with two terrorists blowing themselves up on the morning of the investiture while attempting to fix a bomb to a bridge.

PRINCESS ELIZABETH imprisoned at the Tower in 1554.

IF YOU JOIN the long queues of tourists waiting to gain entrance to the Tower of London today, it is hard to imagine that in previous centuries most people were desperate to stay away from the place. It was a building that struck terror in the hearts of many, especially when they imagined sailing down the Thames in secret and being brought into the tower through Traitor's Gate – a low arched gateway let into the bank of the Thames.

The Tower was begun by William the Conqueror who, after his victory at the Battle of Hastings in 1066, wanted to emphasize his new-found supremacy by erecting a temporary fort outside London's city walls. Later he replaced this fort with a square stone building, which still stands today in the centre of the site. It was then known as the Keep and only became called the White Tower, the name by which it is still known today, when it was whitewashed in 1240. The only entrance was 15 ft above ground, with a set of steps which could be removed in times of crisis.

Successive kings visited the Tower or improved on its fortifications, and the stories concerning them alone would fill a book. Richard I, when he heard that Prince John was plotting to take the throne, had mangonels – special stone-throwing machines – installed, but they did not prevent the Prince from capturing the Tower and taking over the kingdom. In 1215 the Barons, desperate to make King John sign Magna Carta, seized the Tower and offered the throne to the French Dauphin, who stayed here for a year.

Henry III continued the great spate of building and introduced the royal menagerie, which eventually grew to contain leopards from the Holy Roman Emperor, a polar bear from the King of Norway, and an elephant from Louis IX. When Henry married Eleanor of Provence in 1236 the coronation procession set off from the Tower, a practice that was continued by Edward I in 1272.

During the reign of Edward II the defences of the Tower were strengthened – a necessary precaution considering his unpopularity. However, it turned out to be his Queen, Isabella, who was his greatest danger. Edward had imprisoned Roger Mortimer, a rebellious Welsh baron, here in 1322 but Isabella, who was Mortimer's mistress, helped him to escape two years later and in 1326 they seized the Tower, released all the prisoners and handed over the keys to the citizens of London. Edward II was shipped off to Berkeley Castle, where he met a hideous – and much disputed – end in 1327, and Mortimer and Isabella governed the country, while keeping the rightful heir to the throne, Edward III, a prisoner in the Tower. However, supported by the Barons, the young king eventually had Mortimer arrested and executed, and banished his mother to Castle Rising in Norfolk.

As the years passed the history of the Tower became bloodier. Richard II survived the Peasant's Revolt here, and the young Prince James of Scotland was held to ransom here for two years, during which time he became King James I, because his father died on hearing what had happened to his son. The Tower was becoming a place to fear, especially when the Duke of

Exeter, who was Constable of the Tower, introduced the rack in 1446. This instrument of torture became known as the Duke of Exeter's daughter.

The Wars of the Roses added another eventful chapter when the already defeated Henry VI suffered further ignominy by being led into the Tower on an ailing horse with a placard tied to his back. He spent six years as a prisoner in the Wakefield Tower before being rescued by Richard Neville, the Earl of Warwick, and proclaimed King at Westminster. It did not do him much good – he was recaptured at the Battle of Tewkesbury and murdered while saying his prayers in the Wakefield Tower on 21 May 1471.

An infamous story associated with the Tower occurred when the dying Edward IV appointed Richard of Gloucester Protector of his son, the short-lived Edward V. Richard brought the boy to the Tower and persuaded his mother to part with her younger son, the Duke of York, to keep him company. Richard promptly declared the two boys illegitimate and had himself crowned at Westminster, in 1483. The following month, the two boys were murdered in the square tower above Traitor's Gate, until then known as the Garden Tower but ever after called the Bloody Tower. Debate still rages about who was responsible.

However, it was during the reign of Henry VIII and the Reformation of the English Church that the Tower assumed the notoriety for which it is still famous. The list of people executed in the Tower began to grow, and included such notable Tudor figures as Thomas More, John Fisher, Anne Boleyn, Thomas Cromwell and Catherine Howard.

Perhaps the most famous prisoner of all was Princess Elizabeth, the future Elizabeth I, sent to the Tower for two months in 1554 on the orders of her half-sister Mary Tudor when she was incriminated in a plot against Mary. She was released when no further charges could be made against her. When Mary died in 1558 Elizabeth rode from Hatfield to the Tower and, with her customary elegant turn of phrase, patted the ground and said 'Some have fallen from being princes of this land to be prisoners in this place. I am raised from being a prisoner in this place to be prince of the land.'

Today, there is another reason for visiting the Tower of London, and that is to see the Crown Jewels, which have recently been moved to a new Jewel House. Most of them date from the 17th century because much of the regalia was destroyed after Charles I was beheaded in 1649. The oldest objects to have survived the Commonwealth are the Ampulla, in the shape of an eagle, and Spoon, which date from the 14th and 13th centuries respectively. They are used in the coronation ceremony when holy oil is poured from the ampulla on to the spoon and used to anoint the head, breast and palms of the new sovereign.

Finally, there is a legend about the Tower which every visitor knows. If the famous ravens, which live within the walls of the Tower, ever leave, the British Empire will collapse, and so will the Tower. The Empire has long since gone, but the Tower remains and so do the ravens. In fact, they have no choice – their wings are clipped.

THERE HAS BEEN A FORTRESS of some description on the great mound at Windsor since the ancient Britons camped here, but it has been the chief residence of English sovereigns since William the Conqueror was attracted by the prospect of good hunting. He replaced what had been a rough wooden enclosure with a stone wall, but it was Henry III who built the first round tower in 1272. Edward III made more changes to the castle in about 1344, and it became a meeting place for his newly established order of Knights of the Garter. He chose it after reading of a legend that claimed the mound was where King Arthur met his Knights of the Round Table. It is now thought that the Order of the Garter may have been a blind for a witches' coven, of which Edward III was a member, and the blue garter was its emblem.

Whether he practised black magic or not, Edward III carried out considerable building work on the castle, as did other monarchs, including Elizabeth I. St George's Chapel, which is one of the finest Perpendicular buildings in England, was begun by Edward IV, who pulled down most of an earlier chapel to make way for it. It was not finished until after 1519, and ranks second only to Westminster Abbey as a royal mausoleum. The first king to be buried here was, fittingly enough, Edward IV, although all that remains of his tomb (which apparently contained a silver effigy of himself) is a magnificent piece of wrought iron grille. The next king to be buried here, Henry VIII, fared little better. Long before his decaying body reached Windsor it had exploded while the cortège stopped overnight at Syon House and there is a gruesome, though probably apocryphal story, that the royal dogs were found chewing on parts of his stomach the following morning. Whatever the truth of such a tale, Henry was buried next to Jane Seymour as he had commanded, but his splendid bronze and marble tomb was never completed. Charles I was buried in the same grave in 1649, without benefit of any funeral service. Adding to the atmosphere of the chapel, the insignia of the Knights of the Garter hang over the choir stalls.

In 1952, George VI was buried at Windsor with all due ceremony, in a coffin made of Sandringham oak, after lying in state in Westminster Hall, where nearly 300,000 mourners filed past his body. His father, George V, had already been buried there in the family vault and his mother, Queen Mary, joined him there in March 1953.

Yet Windsor is not only connected with royal funerals. It plays a much more important role than that, for not only is the castle a family home – albeit not so emotionally important as Balmoral and Sandringham – but it gave the present family their surname. Although English kings and queens have always had alliances with other countries and have not always been English-born, with the German-speaking George I and the Dutch William of Orange as two prime examples, ill feeling against Germany grew so strong during the First World War that the royal family felt it would be prudent to change their surname from Saxe-Coburg-Gotha (Prince Albert's name) to something quintessentially English. George V was too strongly associated with Germany and his wife, Queen Mary of Teck, spoke with a strong German accent, so he adopted the safe name of Windsor. Not only was it a suitable accompaniment to such other royal dynasties as the Tudors and Plantagenets but it even had a precedent, as Edward III had styled himself Edward of Windsor.

In 1936, Windsor was the obvious choice of title for Edward VIII when he abdicated. Not only was it his family name but he had lived on the outskirts of Windsor Great Park in his adored Fort Belvedere, a place described by Lady Diana Cooper, who was a frequent visitor, as 'a child's idea of a fort'. He had loved it there, giving weekend house parties during which he would lead reluctant guests outside to lend a hand with the gardening. The Duke of York, who was his brother and successor, lived across the park at Royal Lodge, a mansion once owned by the rackety Prince Regent. He and his Duchess worked hard at restoring the house and converting it into a family home, giving it the sort of warm atmosphere that the Duke had missed as a child. Even when he became George VI he would lead his family, guests and all the members of the household into the grounds on Saturdays to work in the woods. He was determined that his two small daughters should grow up in a happy family home, not one constrained by the tensions and shyness that he had known.

In November 1992, the Queen's self-styled *annus horribilis* reached its nadir when Windsor Castle caught fire. Although the castle sustained terrible damage, restoration work has begun and, at the time of writing, much of the castle's contents are being restored to their former glory. While all this is going on, Windsor continues to be open to the public.

THIS FAIRYTALE CASTLE was the favourite retreat of many medieval queens of England and, with its picturesque setting on an island in the middle of a lake, it is easy to see why. It is most closely associated with Henry VIII who turned it from a fortress into a royal palace, but began life under a Saxon, called either Leed or Ledian, who built a wooden fortress here. The castle was rebuilt in stone in 1119 by a Norman knight, and was given to Edward I and his beloved Queen, Eleanor of Castile, in 1278. Edward I increased its fortifications but when he did so could have had no idea that one of the besiegers would be his own son, Edward II. This happened in 1321, after the then owner, Bartholomew, Lord Badlesmere, had joined the 2nd Earl of Lancaster in opposing the King. Huge crossbows, known as 'ballistas', which hurled darts or boulders, were used to attack the castle, which surrendered. All the soldiers inside were either imprisoned or killed.

Witchcraft was always something to be feared, and many women were accused of being witches if they were disliked or strange events connected with them could not be explained in any other way. Joan of Navarre, the widow of Henry IV, was given a three-year prison sentence for witchcraft, and spent the last months of her captivity at Leeds Castle.

However, there is one happy story connected with the castle. It was here that Catherine de Valois, widow of Henry V, fell in love with the man who was to become her second husband, Owen Tudor. At the time, he was her Clerk of the Wardrobe. It was a marriage with important dynastic implications because their son, Edmund Tudor, married his cousin Margaret Beaufort and produced the future Henry VII, thus beginning the rule of the House of Tudor.

Leeds' royal connections are still remembered and celebrated today. Not only is the castle open to the public and full of furniture and artefacts linked to the kings and queens who made this one of their homes, but connections with royalty are still being forged. For example, in 1988 HRH Princess Alexandra, the royal patron of the Leeds Castle Foundation, opened an aviary in the grounds. Other animals are not forgotten, however, as there is even a collection of historic dog collars, including those belonging to many royal canines.

HENRY VIII'S FIRST MEETING with Anne Boleyn in 1522, an engraving of Thomas Stothard's original illustration, the year she became a Lady-in-Waiting to Queen Catherine, Henry VIII's first wife.

I F ANNE BOLEYN were to visit her childhood home of Hever Castle today she would not recognize it, and would wonder why she did not remember the Tudor village that spreads out around the castle itself. It looks authentic enough, but surely . . . ?

In fact, the Tudor village was constructed between 1903 and 1906, at the request of the castle's then owner, William Waldorf Astor, using the same gold and grey sandstone with which the original castle was built. He had the village built because the castle itself was too small to live and entertain in, and although the houses – each one designed to look different – appear to be self-contained they form a network of over 100 rooms, all linked by corridors. To create such a monumental and ingenious piece of building, which was carried out by 800 workmen, the bed of the River Eden and the public road had to be moved. The massive lake was mostly dug by hand by 748 labourers, which is a staggering idea when you gaze out across it today.

Three generations of the Bullen family had lived at Hever when Anne was born, the daughter of Sir Thomas and Lady Elizabeth Bullen. When Anne was a toddler, the eighteen-year-old Henry Tudor was crowned King Henry VIII, and married his first wife, Catherine of Aragon. Anne, whose father was pushy and ambitious on her behalf, spent much of her childhood at Court, then went to France with her father when he was made Ambassador there. By the time they returned to Hever in 1522 Anne was eager for excitement, which she soon found by being made a Lady-in-Waiting to Queen Catherine. However, she fell in love with Lord Henry Percy and was promptly packed off back to Hever, then sent abroad.

By the time she returned her elder sister, Mary, was the King's mistress and her father was basking in the many honours being bestowed on him by Henry. The King himself, however, was not so happy. His once happy marriage to Catherine was becoming soured by her inability to produce a male heir, and her only child to have survived was the infant Princess Mary. Henry needed to ensure the succession and was casting his eye around for another wife. That royal eye fell on Anne. Henry began arriving unannounced at Hever – a habit that sent Lady Elizabeth and her household into a permanent state of turmoil because they never knew when he would appear. Anne was in equal turmoil because Henry first asked her to marry him in 1527, but she replied that she could not be his wife because he already had one, and she would not be his mistress. Determined to marry her, Henry embarked on the 'King's Great Matter' – the knotty problem of how he could divorce Catherine and marry Anne. He solved it by disassociating himself from the Roman Catholic Church and founding the Church of England, with himself as head. It was the start of the Reformation – the conversion of Britain from a Catholic country to a Protestant one.

Henry's divorce was on the way at last, but he felt unable to wait until it was finalised and married Anne secretly on 25 January 1533 at Whitehall Palace. In May of the same year the divorce was announced and Henry's marriage to Catherine declared invalid. By now Anne's name had changed three times – firstly from Bullen to the more aristocratic sounding Boleyn, then to Lady Anne Rochford (her father had been created Viscount Rochford by Henry) and thirdly to the Marquess of Pembroke (both men and women were called Marquess at this time). On 1 June 1533 at Westminster, her name changed again, to the most sumptuous title of all – Queen Anne.

By now Anne was pregnant, and Henry was confident that he had done the right thing in marrying her. The arrival of his son and heir presumptive was eagerly awaited and on 7 September Anne gave birth at Greenwich Palace – to a baby girl. It was a bitter disappointment. The child was named Princess Elizabeth, and Anne was soon pregnant again. Yet her second pregnancy ended in miscarriage and, in a final ironic twist that cannot have gone unnoticed by the King, she miscarried again (the foetus was male) on 29 January 1536 – the day of Catherine of Aragon's funeral.

That day sounded not only the death knell of Catherine but of Anne herself. The King had run out of patience and was rapidly running out of time. He was desperate to have an heir, and needed to find a way to get rid of Anne so he could marry her Lady-in-Waiting, Jane Seymour. On 1 May five men, including Anne's brother George, Lord Rochford, were arrested for being her lovers and the following day Anne herself was sent to the Tower on the charge of high treason, accused of committing adultery with those same men. Henry moved fast. Anne and her brother were tried and found guilty of incest on 15 May, while the other four men had been found guilty of adultery and therefore treason the day before. This was hardly surprising, as in those days anyone accused of treason was not allowed to have a defending counsel. Both Anne's uncle, the Duke of Norfolk, and her father declared their belief in Anne's guilt – they had to, if they wanted to save their own necks, otherwise they would have been condemned to death through association. Anne's so-called lovers were all executed on 17 May and two days later Anne met the same fate herself, within the walls of the Tower on Tower Green. She had asked to be executed with a sword instead of an axe, and a skilled swordsman was sent from Calais specially for the purpose.

It was recorded by Sir William Kingston, then Governor of the Tower, that he had watched most people going to their executions in fear, but that Anne had 'much joy and pleasure in death'. As she stood on the scaffold she said 'I am not here to preach to you but to die. Pray for the King, for he is a good man and has treated me as good could be. I do not accuse anyone of causing my death, neither the judges nor anyone else for I am condemned by the law of the land and die willingly.' After she was beheaded, her body was thrown into an old arrow chest, which served as her coffin. She was buried in the chapel of St Peter ad Vincula, within the walls of the Tower. Anne of a Thousand Days had ended her reign. On 30 May 1536, eleven days after Anne's execution, Henry married his third wife, Jane Seymour, at Whitehall Palace.

Anne Boleyn is the Queen most commonly associated with Hever Castle, and she certainly has the strongest link. Yet another of Henry VIII's wives also lived here. Anne's father died in 1538 and Henry, ever eager to acquire whatever took his fancy, appropriated Hever Castle for himself. It came in very useful two years later. Henry was wondering what to do about his fourth wife, Anne of Cleves, whom he had just divorced after six months of unconsummated marriage. He had married her for political reasons, at the suggestion of Thomas Cranmer, and also because he had been bewitched by a Holbein portrait of her. However, when he finally met the 'Flanders Mare', as he was alleged to have called her, he realised the portrait had been highly flattering and was apparently struck dumb – but not by love.

Anne of Cleves had the luckiest escape of any of Henry's wives as she lived happily at Hever Castle for the next seventeen years until her death in 1557. She even remained on good terms with the quick-tempered King. With his customary rapidity, Henry embarked on his fifth marriage on 28 July 1540, the same month that his divorce from Anne of Cleves was announced. This time he married Catherine Howard, a cousin of Anne Boleyn's and a Lady-in-Waiting of Anne of Cleves. History, however, was about to repeat itself. Like her cousin, Catherine met exactly the same fate and for the same reason of adultery. The only difference is that this time Henry's wife was probably guilty as charged.

Fᴀᴍɪʟʏ ʟɪꜰᴇ is not always as easy and harmonious as one might wish, yet relationships rarely degenerate to such a poor state that they end in pitched battles. It is a different story in royal families, however, because for every happy filial relationship there is one that ends in abdication, bloodshed or murder. Even the quiet county town of Lewes has experienced a battle for power waged between brothers-in-law.

Like his father, King John, Henry III was a despotic king but unfortunately he was also an ineffectual one – a dire and dangerous combination. After losing battles and land in France, Henry needed to replenish the royal coffers so asked his barons for the money. In 1258 they agreed to his request, on the proviso that he accepted some important reforms which would establish a privy council to rule the country and counter arbitrary royal rule. However, Henry reneged on the agreement and sparked off the Barons' War, led by his brother-in-law, Simon de Montfort. The two sides met at Lewes in May 1264, with Henry's son, Prince Edward (who became Edward I on his father's death) fighting on the King's side. However, the Prince was not much help because he mounted a cavalry charge which removed him from

the scene of the battle for two hours. In his absence, his father was captured by the enemy, and remained in the barons' hands for the next fifteen months. Edward was also detained by his uncle, but managed to escape in June 1265. He raised an army and fought de Montfort in August of that year at the Battle of Evesham. Royalist troops outnumbered the baronial troops by two to one, and the battle was nothing less than a bloodbath. De Montfort was killed and power returned to the throne, although Edward was the effective ruler. By now Henry was senile, and Edward succeeded to the throne in 1272.

The Norman keep of Lewes Castle, where Edward stayed before the Battle of Lewes, is still standing, although most of the castle was restored in the 19th century. Lewes has another royal link in Anne of Cleves' house, which is tucked away in the medieval suburb of Southover. Originally the house was part of Lewes Priory, but it became the property of the Crown during the Dissolution of the Monasteries in 1540 and in due course was given to Anne of Cleves by Henry VIII as part of her divorce settlement. She never lived there, but she enjoyed the revenue that the house brought her.

THIS IS ONE OF THE MOST perfect-looking castles in Britain, and is immaculately preserved and extremely impressive. It was built just after the Norman Conquest by Roger Montgomery, Earl of Shrewsbury, who wanted a fortress to stand guard over the vulnerable Arun valley that stretches down to the South Coast and the English Channel. Further additions to the fortress were made in 1170 and 1190.

In 1290 the then owner, Richard Fitzalan, was made Earl of Arundel, and his family continued to own the castle until 1580, when the last Earl – Henry, the 12th Earl – died without a male heir. His daughter, Mary, had married Thomas Howard, the 4th Duke of Norfolk (the premier Duke of England), who was executed for treason in 1572. The Dukedom was forfeited but his grandson, Thomas, was awarded the title once more by James I in 1604. Thomas was greatly trusted by James' son, Charles I, and in 1642, at the start of the Civil War, he escorted Queen Henrietta Maria to the Continent while war raged in England. Not only was Charles I one of the casualties of the war but so was Arundel Castle, first falling to the Roundheads and then being recaptured by the Royalists. The Roundheads returned in 1644 and fired a cannon from the top of the nearby church which nearly destroyed the barbican.

The Dukedom of Norfolk was restored to the family yet again in 1660 by Charles II, although the castle had been so badly damaged during the Civil War that it was not until 1787 that it was considered habitable.

Queen Victoria came here to visit the 13th Duke in 1846, but he was so worried about her reaction to the stained glass window in the dining room, which showed Solomon entertaining the Queen of Sheba, that he had it removed before she arrived.

The Dukes of Norfolk are also the Earl Marshalls of England, and as such are required to manage all State processions and ceremonies, as well as preside over the College of Arms. The 16th Duke of Norfolk arranged the celebrations for George V's Silver Jubilee, the funerals of George V and George VI, and the coronations of George VI and his daughter, Elizabeth II.

If you walk or drive through Arundel you will be hard pressed not to see the castle. It dominates the pretty town and stands tall and proud on a chalk spur above the River Arun. Swans glide serenely along the river, adding to the charm of the view and making passing tourists reach for their cameras. The castle itself is so perfectly preserved and maintained that walking around it is curiously like being Alice in Wonderland in a toy fort. The keep and barbican were renovated between 1870 and 1890, but blend in wonderfully with the original 12th-century parts of the castle. Bibliophiles should make straight for the Gothick library, which is cosily welcoming with its mahogany carvings, galleries and ceiling, and the red and gold stripes of the carpet. As for the books – there are ten thousand of them and although they cannot be removed from their shelves they nevertheless contribute to the powerfully inviting atmosphere of the room. Its design was intended to resemble a church, and the room certainly has an air of bibliophilic worship.

LADY ELIZABETH BOWES-LYON, the future Queen Mother, poses by an old cannon at her family home, Glamis Castle, in 1932.

GLAMIS CASTLE, owned by the Earls of Strathmore and Kinghorne, is the stuff of legend. It has all the ingredients of Gothic romance, not only being the place where royalty has been born, lived and died, but also apparently being the most haunted house in Scotland and even having its very own monster.

According to legend, if you count the windows on the outside of the castle you will find there is one more than if you were to count them on the inside. That is because one of the windows belongs to the secret chamber in which a hideously deformed creature – more like a toad than a man, it is reported – was born two hundred years ago. The story says that as each heir to the earldom of Strathmore and Kinghorne came of age he would be taken to the secret chamber and shown the rightful earl – a most gruesome experience, by all accounts. Apparently this horrific beast only died in the 1920s, and its demise must have come as an immense relief to the family, the Bowes-Lyons.

Malcolm III is traditionally said to have died here and the ghost of Macbeth is said to haunt the castle, endlessly bemoaning Duncan's death. James V ordered the execution of the widow of the 6th Lord Glamis and her second husband, claiming they had tried to murder him through witchcraft. Lady Glamis' son, the 7th Lord, was imprisoned in Edinburgh Castle, to await his own execution, and Glamis was declared forfeit to the Crown. James V enjoyed visiting Glamis, although after his death the castle passed out of royal hands and ownership returned to the 7th Lord.

The Old Pretender, who was the son of James II and was recognized by Jacobites as James III of England and James VIII of Scotland, lodged here in 1715, and the son of the 5th Earl died fighting for his cause at Sherrifmuir. But the most recent royal connection for Glamis is that the 14th Earl of Strathmore and Kinghorne's youngest daughter, Lady Elizabeth Bowes-Lyon, married the Duke of York in 1923. They spent part of their honeymoon here. The Duke subsequently, and unexpectedly, became George VI after his brother, Edward VIII, abdicated. Princess Margaret was born here in 1926 – the first member of the immediate royal family to have been born in Scotland since 1602.

There are two huge lures that draw visitors to Glamis each year. The first is the magnetic attraction caused by its being the Queen Mother's childhood home and the birthplace of Princess Margaret. The other fascination of Glamis is its impressive catalogue of ghosts and, of course, that hideous monster. The castle is so atmospheric that even the most hard-headed visitor might sometimes be forgiven for imagining that they will accidentally (and terrifyingly) stumble across the hidden room in which one Earl Beardie endlessly plays dice with the Devil – his punishment for gambling on a Sunday.

And then there are the visitors who come to Glamis for the sheer beauty of the place. For the long avenue of trees in the drive, for the warmth and intimacy of the public rooms – because Glamis is still a family home – and the impressive collections of paintings and porcelain, Glamis has something to offer everyone.

CATHERINE OF ARAGON died at Kimbolton Castle on 7 January 1536. It was rumoured that Henry VIII had poisoned her.

THIS TUDOR MANOR HOUSE was the enforced residence of Catherine of Aragon in the 1530s, not a time she can have thought of with any great affection, despite the religious piety she had adopted by then. She was held here by Sir Richard Wingfield, a confidant of her divorced husband, Henry VIII, and she died here in 1536.

All things considered, Catherine was lucky to die of natural causes, even if the last four years of her life were spent in seclusion. She was born in 1485, the year when the English throne changed from the Yorkist dynasty to the Tudors, and was the fourth daughter of Ferdinand II and Isabella of Spain, the royal supporters of Christopher Columbus' voyages around the globe. Her future father-in-law, Henry VII, was skilled at uniting warring factions through marriage – he was a Lancastrian who had effectively ended the Wars of the Roses by marrying Elizabeth of York, and he arranged for his daughter Mary to marry Louis XII of France and for another daughter, Margaret, to marry James IV of Scotland. He saw the young Catherine as the ideal way of bringing Britain and Spain together and arranged for her to marry his eldest son, Arthur, in 1501. However, Arthur died of consumption five months later. Henry VII was reluctant to lose such a good connection with Spain and arranged for Catherine to become betrothed to her brother-in-law, Henry VII's second son and heir apparent, Henry. But Henry was a mere boy, being only eleven at the time, and they had to wait. They were married in 1509, six weeks after the death of Henry VII, and Catherine finally became Queen of England.

Sadly, it did not do her much good. Henry VIII was desperate for an heir and although Catherine gave birth to five children, including a son in 1511, only their daughter Princess Mary survived. By 1527, Henry was convinced that such misfortune was caused by God's displeasure with him for marrying his dead brother's widow, and was anxious to rid himself of her as soon as possible. Once he did so and married Anne Boleyn, he reasoned, he would immediately start producing a string of healthy sons. In those days of such high rates of infant mortality, problems such as infertility or a lack of sons were always considered to be the fault of the woman, not the man.

Henry told Cardinal Wolsey to arrange a papal annulment of the marriage, but Pope Clement was reluctant to oblige and the matter dragged on for years. By 1529 Henry had lost patience with Wolsey and subsequently had him arrested for high treason but, mercifully for him, Wolsey died on his way to London in 1530. Thomas Cromwell took his place as Henry's chief minister and devised a way to rid Henry of his unwanted Queen and marry Anne Boleyn, with whom he was by then in love. Cromwell suggested that Henry should stage a formal breach with the Pope, and then the Primate of England, Archbishop Cranmer, would be able to declare Henry's marriage to Catherine null and void. Henry secretly married the pregnant Anne Boleyn on 25 January 1533 at Whitehall Palace and divorced Catherine in May of the same year. The following year Henry was excommunicated by the Pope and declared by Parliament to be 'the supreme head on earth of the English Church'. So began his Reformation, which was to have such profound effects on Britain.

If poor Catherine of Aragon were to revisit Kimbolton today it is doubtful if she would recognize the place. What was a Tudor manor house has become a showpiece for the talents of Sir John Vanbrugh and Nicholas Hawksmoor, who were commissioned to remodel the building in the early 18th century. It contains murals by Pellegrini. The gatehouse was designed by Robert Adam but it is not known whether the sight of it strikes pleasure or dismay in the hearts of Kimbolton's 20th-century inhabitants – it is now a school. Nevertheless, it is open to the public during some school holidays.

QUEEN VICTORIA at Balmoral with her beloved gillie, John Brown.

ORIGINALLY, IN THE 15TH CENTURY, the castle known today as Balmoral was called Bouchmorale – Gaelic for 'majestic dwelling'. Anyone looking at the castle today will understand why it was given that name, although the present building was largely rebuilt by Queen Victoria and her beloved consort, Prince Albert, after they bought the estate in 1852. It was love at first sight for the Queen, who first saw her future Scottish residence in 1848, when she bought the lease. It was a place where, she said, 'all seemed to breathe freedom and peace'.

Balmoral looks like a toy, a child's idea of what a castle should be. It is built of granite in Scots baronial style, and has layers of turrets and a massive east tower which gives superb views of the surrounding countryside. Prince Albert paid £31,000 for the castle and the rebuilding programme took three years. It was a good investment, because the royal family have spent the late summers here ever since, enjoying the shooting that makes Scotland so popular in August and September and the beautiful scenery in a part of Grampian that has become known as Royal Deeside.

Queen Victoria was especially fond of Balmoral, and her second ever train journey took her to Scotland and her new home. She adored it, partly because she loved Scotland and partly because of the work lavished on the place by her husband. She was happiest of all here. 'Every year', she wrote, 'my heart becomes more fixed in this dear Paradise, and so much more so now, that all has become my dear Albert's *own* creation, own work, own building, own laying-out; – and his great taste, and the impress of his dear hand, have been stamped everywhere.'

Edward VII enjoyed the shooting here, although his grandson, Edward VIII, saw the place as a reminder of the stuffy family life he was trying so hard to shake off. During the fateful year of 1936, when Britain was to have three kings, he decided to hold a house party at Balmoral in August and September. That was following royal tradition, yet he chose Mrs Simpson to be his hostess, and caused considerable offence not only to the household but also to nearby Aberdeen. Some months before he had been asked to open some new hospital buildings in Aberdeen, but had refused on the grounds that he was still in mourning for his father.

Mourning had not, however, prevented him attending Ascot that June, nor did it prevent him suggesting that his brother, the then Duke of York, should open the hospital in his place. The Aberdonians found that upsetting enough, as surely the period of mourning would have applied to the King's brothers as well as himself, but the final snub came on the very day of the Duke of York's visit to Aberdeen, when a royal car was seen driving to the station to collect Mrs Simpson and her friends. The driver was none other than the King himself.

A much happier event took place at Balmoral in the late summer of 1946 when Prince Philip, on leave from the Navy, proposed to the then Princess Elizabeth. Although there was considerable debate about when the young Prince Philip of Greece should renounce his Greek nationality – Greece at that time was locked in civil war and his marriage to an English princess promised to be a source of potential embarrassment for the royal family – he became impatient at waiting for government ministers to decide his future happiness and took matters into his own hands. Even so, the couple were told that although they could consider themselves engaged, they were not allowed to make the news public, and it was not until 10 July 1947 that the official announcement came from Buckingham Palace. In the meantime, Prince Philip of Greece had become a naturalized British citizen. His surname had caused lengthy debate, because Schleswig-Holstein-Sonderburg-Glucksburg was considered far too German for comfort. The College of Heralds was set to work to find a suitable name from his ancestry, and came up with Oldenburg, which they suggested might be changed to Oldcastle. Eventually, Mountbatten was chosen, as acknowledgement of his mother's maiden name of Battenberg, and the Prince took his new name of Lieutenant Philip Mountbatten. Ironically enough, all this anxiety about his naturalization had proved unnecessary because by this time it had been realized that the Act of Settlement of 1701, which excluded Catholic Stuarts from any claim to the British throne, had given British nationality and royal status to all descendants of the Electress Sophia of Hanover. As Prince Philip was one of these it turned out that he had been a British prince all the time.

V IRTUALLY EVERY STORY that surrounds the semi-
legendary King Arthur is an amalgam of vague fact
and romantic embroidery, including the ones concerning
his sword. According to Sir Thomas Malory's *Morte
d'Arthur*, Arthur drew a magic sword out of an anvil (the
sword in the stone) – a feat which no other man had been
able to achieve. Victory was always assured with the sword,
but when it was broken in battle Arthur was given a
replacement, the famed Excalibur. It was forged in the
mysterious Isle of Avalon (now believed to be Glastonbury
Tor) and enabled Arthur to slay 940 Saxons at the battle of
Mount Badon. After Arthur was wounded at the Battle of
Camlann, Excalibur was said to have been thrown by
Bedevere into Dozmary Pool (see right) on Bodmin
Moor. This vast sheet of water, more of a lake than a pool,
was believed to be bottomless, although it has been known
to dry out in hot summers.

STROLLERS IN EPPING FOREST today might like to remember that they are walking through a part of England that has been afforested since the Iron Age. There is a hill fort at Ambersbury Banks which is said to have been used by Boadicea. She objected strongly when Roman troops seized the Norfolk and Suffolk land of her husband, Prasutagus, after his death in AD 60. She joined forces with the Trinovantes and took London, but after she was defeated in battle near Epping Forest the following year she and her daughters committed suicide by eating poisonous berries.

An abbey, from which the area known as Waltham Abbey takes its name, was founded in the forest in 1030, and in 1060 it was rebuilt by King Harold. Six years later he prayed here on his way to Hastings to fight the invading Normans. He lost the battle and was buried in the abbey.

Harold was not the only king to visit the abbey, and many monarchs enjoyed hunting in the forest. In 1226 Henry III ordained that Londoners should be allowed to hunt in the forest once a year, on Easter Monday, and this became a great occasion.

Waltham Abbey suffered the fate of all other monastic foundations in 1540, during Henry VIII's Dissolution of the Monasteries, although part of the Norman nave survived the destruction and was amalgamated in the building of the new parish church.

Hunting was no longer a keen royal pursuit by the 17th century and it was highwaymen who hunted in the forest instead. William III narrowly escaped being a highwayman's prey in 1698, but it is not recorded whether this was because the highwayman wanted rich pickings or whether he was a supporter of James II, whom William had deposed in 1688 during the Glorious Revolution. James' pro-Catholic reforms and conversion to Catholicism, followed by the birth of his son James (the future Old Pretender) in 1688, sent shock waves of alarm through Britain. It was easy to imagine what would happen if James remained on the throne – there would be a re-run of Mary I's Catholic reign, with all the terror and bloodshed that had accompanied it, and the prospect of a continuation of such misery when the young James succeeded. The Protestant Prince William of Orange was invited to take over the British throne and he duly arrived at Torbay, accompanied by an invasion force. Both he and his wife Mary were entitled to succeed to the throne – William was the grandson of Charles I, but Mary had an even stronger claim, being the daughter of James II. She had overthrown her own father.

LAPPED BY THE TIDE which leaves small boats stranded on mud flats during its daily retreats, the pretty village of Bosham (pronounced *bozzum*) stands on the shoreline of one of the many creeks in Chichester Harbour. If you stroll around it today you might be forgiven for thinking that its chief claim to fame is its photogenic quality, yet Bosham twice played a significant role in medieval history. It was also an important harbour for ships sailing to France and beyond.

During the reign of the Danish King Canute, or Cnut, in the early 11th century, he was profoundly irritated by his courtiers who expected him to be all-powerful. To prove otherwise, he sat in a chair on the sand at Bosham and commanded the incoming tide to come to a halt. It continued merrily on its way, wetting his feet and legs, so he said, 'Let all men know how empty and worthless is the power of kings, for there is none worthy of the name, but He whom heaven, earth and sea obey by eternal laws.'

In 1064 Bosham featured in an event which was depicted in the Bayeux Tapestry. Harold, Earl of Wessex (who became King Harold II on the death of Edward the Confessor in January 1066) was about to set sail from Bosham to visit Duke William of Normandy, to confirm King Edward's promise that the French duke would be next in line to the throne and swear an oath to that effect. First, Harold prayed at Bosham church, then set sail for France. In the event, when Edward died on 5 January 1066, Harold was crowned the following day. An incensed Duke William, plus an outraged King of Norway, who had also been promised the English throne, both set sail to fight for their right to the crown. And the rest, as they say, is history.

LIKE SO MANY KINGS, William the Conqueror loved hunting. He had made the English crown his, and Winchester his capital, and his next requirement was to have somewhere nearby to hunt to his heart's content. He chose a large area of scrubland to the west of Southampton which had been Ytene, a favourite hunting ground of Saxon kings. Planting began in 1079, and Lyndhurst, in the centre of the forest, was created a royal manor.

William wanted to protect his royal hunting ground and ensure that the precious deer who lived in it were undisturbed by local villagers, so he introduced a series of pernicious laws that ensured anyone caught disturbing the deer would be blinded, and anyone who killed a deer would be put to death himself.

Death came to the New Forest, but it was in a famous case of presumed regicide. After William the Conqueror died in 1087 his son, William Rufus (so-named because of his ruddy complexion) assumed the throne. He was responsible for the building of Westminster Hall, so history has cause to thank him, but the events that took place near Lyndhurst in the New

Forest on 2 August 1100 cast severe doubts on his popularity during his lifetime. At the end of a day's hunting, while William and his seven companions were waiting to make their last kill, a stag ran between them. Walter Tirel, a knight, fired at the stag with his arrow but missed, and killed the king instead. Contemporary accounts claimed that Walter Tirel always denied the whole story, saying that not only had he not fired the fatal arrow but that he had not been out hunting that day. If it was not an accident, then it was regicide, and throughout history the finger of blame has pointed at one man – William's brother Henry. He seized the throne although, being William the Conqueror's third son, he was not the heir apparent – the true heir, Robert Curthose of Normandy, was returning from the First Crusade at the time.

William died on a Thursday evening and his body was brought to Henry at Winchester the following morning. He was buried in the cathedral that same day, and Henry paused only to seize the Treasury before riding with all speed to London and his coronation that very Sunday. It was suspicious behaviour, to say the least.

THE WILD INHOSPITABLE SCENERY of Glencoe is an appropriate testament to the savagery that took place there in February 1692, the result of terrible feuds waged between the Highland clans and the English government which was failing to keep them under control. William III and Mary II were on the throne but had to combat a swelling Jacobite cause, which aimed to return the deposed James II (Mary's father) to what they saw as his rightful position as King. They had no desire to be ruled by a Dutchman who had little interest in Scotland and who was unpopular anyway.

In an effort to put the Scots in their place, the Government announced that all Highland chiefs should swear an oath of allegiance to the Crown by 1 January 1692, but the MacDonalds of Glencoe were not able to do so until six days later. It was decided that an example should be made of the clan, so Argyll troops headed by Captain Robert Campbell (who bore a long-standing grudge against the MacDonalds) arrived in Glencoe on 1 February and asked for

shelter. They were received with true Highland hospitality, despite the fact that the two clans were traditional enemies. Campbell had been ordered to kill every man under seventy but his ineptitude meant this attempt at mass-murder was bungled when his soldiers suddenly launched their fierce attack on their hosts at dawn on 13 February. Over 38 people were slaughtered, while many others who fled to the surrounding mountains were killed by the treacherous conditions they found there.

Wherever the story was told it was greeted with revulsion and horror. The Government troops had committed 'murder under trust', and had broken the greatest unwritten Scots law of all, that of hospitality. William III's reputation, which had been less than rosy before Glencoe, was ruined for ever after the massacre took place, because it was his signature that had been on the order to murder the MacDonalds. Whether or not he knew what the order contained, he was ultimately responsible.

ON A HOT SUMMER'S DAY, when Iona is crammed with sightseers, it can be difficult to think of this tiny island off the coast of Mull as being a haven of peace and tranquillity. Yet after a while you begin to understand why it has always been considered a holy island.

The Druids had built a temple here long before St Columba arrived to build his monastery in AD 563 and bring Christianity to the Western Isles of Scotland. Invading Vikings sacked the monastery several times and massacred the monks, but the community continued to survive through the centuries, and sixty kings were buried here. Among them was Duncan I, who died fighting his cousin, a rival claimant to the Scots throne, on 1 August 1040. The victor of the battle was Macbeth, and after killing Duncan he ruled for seventeen years until one of Duncan's sons, Malcolm, invaded Scotland in 1054 with the backing of the English King, Edward the Confessor, and the military help of Earl Siward of Northumberland. Malcolm fought Macbeth in Aberdeenshire and won, but the King fled north. He was finally killed by Malcolm on 15 August 1057. Macbeth's stepson, Lulach, assumed the Scottish throne but was killed in an ambush the following year. Both he and Macbeth were buried on Iona.

Malcolm Canmore was crowned Malcolm III, King of all Scotland, on 25 April 1058 and launched a dynasty, the House of Dunkeld, which lasted for three centuries. Malcolm first married Ingibjorg, the widow of Earl Thorfinn II of Orkney, which strengthened Scotland's ties with the Scandinavians in the north of the country, then married Margaret, an English princess. This forged strong links (which were desperately needed) between Scotland and England and St Margaret, as she became known after her death, introduced many English customs and some civilizing influences into a country that was still barbaric in many ways.

The last king to be buried on Iona was Donald III, the brother of Malcolm III and his successor to the throne. Donald was deposed twice and faced bitter opposition from Malcolm's sons. Duncan II, son of Malcolm and Ingibjorg, deposed Donald in 1094 but was killed by his uncle at the end of that year. After Donald's death in 1097 Malcolm's three sons by Margaret reigned successively – Edgar, Alexander I and David I.

DUNFERMLINE ABBEY is second only to Iona as a burial place of Scottish kings and queens, and the town of Dunfermline was the Scottish capital for six hundred years. Queen Margaret and King Malcolm III are buried here, as are David I and his two queens, Robert the Bruce and several other medieval monarchs.

Strangely enough, for a man who was one of the great heroes of Scotland, Robert the Bruce's burial place was forgotten for many years and was only discovered during building work in 1818. A skeleton was found, wrapped in a shroud made from cloth-of-gold, and its identity was confirmed by its severed breastbone. This was because Robert the Bruce had declared that, after his death, he wanted his heart to be taken to the Holy Land by his friend, Lord James Douglas. Obligingly, Douglas took the heart with him, in a silver casket, on his next crusade to Spain and threw it at the Saracens, shouting that it should go first as it had always done. Douglas was killed in the fighting, but Robert the Bruce's heart was brought back to Scotland and now lies under the floor of Melrose Abbey.

It was the marriage of Malcolm Canmore to Queen Margaret in 1070 which first put Dunfermline on the map, and the King then lived in a tower nearby. In 1075 Queen Margaret ordered the laying of the foundations of the Benedictine priory, which was raised to an abbey by David I in the 12th century. The nave of the present abbey dates from this time, although the rest of the abbey fell into decay over the centuries. This process was speeded up in 1303

when Edward I (described in the 16th century as the Hammer of the Scots) held court within the abbey and had most of the buildings burned when he left the following year. Protestant Reformers also attacked the abbey in 1560, but left the nave, which served as the parish church until the new church was built in 1821.

The palace, which was the guest house of the abbey, was very large, but only a little of it remains today. Charles I was born here on 19 November 1600, and its last royal tenant was Charles II, who stayed here just before the Battle of Pitreavie, in July 1650.

Dunfermline Abbey can be visited all year round, even though little evidence remains of its illustrious past. The guest house which served as the palace has crumbled away until only a wall, tower and archway still stand, and you can see the nave of the old abbey, but for the rest you must rely on your imagination. Inspect the graves, many of which are inscribed with names straight out of the history books, and try to imagine what the abbey must have been like during its medieval heyday.

Pittencrief Park stands beside the abbey and was bought, along with Pittencrief House, by Andrew Carnegie for the town. He was the son of a local weaver but emigrated to America in 1848. Once there his fortunes took a definite turn for the better – as a steel magnate he became the richest man in the world and also one of the most generous, giving away a cool $350 million during his lifetime.

A SIMPLE STONE SLAB in the middle of a stretch of grassland marks the spot where King Harold was killed during the Battle of Hastings. What the memorial does not say is that this is where Saxon England also died, and Norman England began. The Battle of Hastings was the culmination of the last successful invasion of Britain, and it had a radical impact on all aspects of British life.

The year 1066 was a landmark in British history, not only because of the battle. It was a year in which there were three English kings on the throne (a phenomenon repeated in 1483 and again in 1936). The year began with the ailing Edward the Confessor still clinging on to life, but he died, after a reign of 23 years, on 5 January 1066. The problem was who could succeed him, because he had no direct heirs. Edward had spent many years of his reign exiled in Norman France (the home of his mother) while the Danish King Canute and his two sons ruled England, and when he returned to the throne his pro-Norman views had not met with full approval in England. Nevertheless, in return for Norman support Edward promised the throne to William, 7th Duke of Normandy in 1051, but when he was dying he changed his mind and named his brother-in-law, Harold, Earl of Wessex, as his successor. As if matters were not complicated enough, there was a third contender to the throne – King Harold Hardrada of Norway – who claimed that his father, Magnus, had made a treaty with Hardecanute when he ruled England. Just to add a little spice, King Harold Hardrada was the half-brother of Harold, Earl of Wessex. The stage was set for a mighty battle.

Anxious not to waste any time in case it was used by the rival claimants, Harold had himself crowned King Harold II at Westminster Abbey on 6 January 1066, but he did not occupy the throne for very long. There was a brief skirmish in May when Harold's younger brother Tostig landed with his forces in an attempt to take the throne, but they were trounced. The next challenge came in early September, when King Harold Hardrada of Norway landed in northern England, accompanied by over 300 ships carrying his troops. English forces led by Harold II marched up to Yorkshire and defeated the Norwegians soundly at the Battle of Stamford Bridge on 25 September. Harold was still celebrating this victory when news came that William, Duke of Normandy, had set sail from France to claim the English throne, with full Papal authority to do so.

Harold gathered together his troops and marched them south, arriving at an area of land now known as Battle on the evening of 13 October. His men were tired and footsore, whereas William's troops, who had only marched from nearby Pevensey, were strong and rested. The fighting began at nine o'clock the following morning on Senlac Hill, with the English troops on foot and about a third of the Normans on horseback. The English were formidable opponents because of their crack troops, the housecarls, who wielded vicious two-handed battleaxes. However, victory was not to be theirs – in early evening Harold was hacked down by a Norman knight (not, as is popularly believed, shot through the eye) and the English troops surrendered. Harold was buried on the seashore at Pevensey, where the Norman troops had come ashore (although later reburied at Waltham Abbey), and William was crowned King of England at Westminster Abbey on 25 December 1066.

About four years later William announced that an abbey should be built on the site of the battle to commemorate the soldiers who had died. In terms of propaganda this was a good move because it showed his piety, but it was also astute politically because it would lead to the population of a part of Sussex which had proved all too easy to invade – he did not want anyone to follow his example and succeed. William ordained that the high altar should be placed on the exact spot where Harold had died, but the monks who were to construct the abbey were appalled at the prospect of having to build on a narrow ridge of land with no water supply. Nevertheless, they followed orders and the abbey was consecrated in 1094 and endowed by William to such a lavish extent that it was one of the richest religious foundations in England.

The Dissolution of the Monasteries spelt the end of Battle Abbey, and in August 1538 the buildings and much of the land were given by Henry VIII to his friend, Sir Anthony Browne. Sir Anthony demolished part of the abbey, including the church, and built a guest house in case his royal charges, Prince Edward and Princess Elizabeth, wished to visit him. The abbey was owned by the Browne family until 1715 when it was sold, and successive owners enlarged and adapted the buildings. Part of the abbey was leased to a school after the First World War, and the original 11th-century buildings are still being excavated.

OF ALL THE EVENTS that have taken place in this beautiful and historic cathedral over the past one thousand fourteen hundred years, one stands out above all the others, and that is the murder of St Thomas à Becket on 29 December 1170.

At the time of his death, Becket was Archbishop of Canterbury, and fiercely opposed to Henry II's attempts to limit the power of the Church. The two men were friends, but Becket had been so anxious to prove his independence from the Crown that he had opposed many of Henry's reforms and become a real thorn in the King's side. Becket was exiled for five years but returned in 1170, scandalized that Henry's surviving eldest son, Henry the Young King, had been crowned while his father was still alive. As Archbishop, he believed that the people responsible should be punished, and when word of this reached Henry he responded with exasperation, asking 'Who will rid me of this turbulent priest?' It was more of a rhetorical question than a royal request, but four knights accepted the challenge with alacrity. As Henry was busy curbing the nobles' powers at the time, they no doubt wanted to curry favour with him. News of the murder in the cathedral sent shockwaves through the Christian world, and Becket was canonized two years later. On 12 July 1174, a barefoot Henry walked into Canterbury to do penance for the murder. He was scourged by the monks as he walked to Becket's tomb, and spent the night there in vigil. It was probably a political move as much as a religious one, because Henry wanted to appear to be contrite and also wanted to pray for victory in the two wars he was waging at the time – in Northumberland against the invading Scots, and in Aquitaine. He had his wish with the former war because the Scots King, William the Lion, was captured and relinquished his claim to Northumberland.

Henry II's grandson, Henry III, was married at Canterbury Cathedral to Eleanor of Provence on 20 January 1236, and another marriage took place just under four hundred years later. This was the wedding of the ill-fated Charles I to Henrietta Maria, sister of King Louis XIII of France. They had already been married by proxy on 1 May 1625, but the marriage was solemnized on 13 June at Canterbury Cathedral. Although the couple were very happy together after a shaky start, their marriage ended in tragedy, with Henrietta Maria escaping to Paris and Charles being executed for treason.

Charles was secretly buried in St George's Chapel, Windsor Castle, in the same grave as Henry VIII, but Canterbury is the final resting place of three royal figures – Henry IV, his wife Joan of Navarre and Edward, the Black Prince.

AN ANNOTATED ENGRAVING showing the cycle of events at Boscobel House when Charles II hid in a oak tree before escaping to France.

THE CITY OF WORCESTER is renowned for its medieval buildings, but the cathedral is the most stunning of all. It was built on the site of a monastery founded by St Oswald in AD 983, and work on the cathedral began in 1084 at the instigation of Wulstan who was Bishop at the time. It was three hundred years before the cathedral was finished, but in the meantime it had attracted plenty of royal notice. King John's will expressed the desire to be buried 'in the Church of the Blessed Virgin and St Wulstan at Worcester', and his body was brought here from Newark Castle and placed in a tomb in front of the High Altar. The marble figure of the King is said to be the oldest royal effigy in England.

As the building of the cathedral progressed, dungeons were installed. They soon had a royal occupant – John's son and successor, Henry III, who was imprisoned here after his defeat by Simon de Montfort at the Battle of Lewes in 1264.

Worcester is perhaps most famous for the battle which took place here on 3 September 1651 during the Civil War, when Oliver Cromwell's Roundheads fought the army of Charles II. Charles' father, Charles I, had been executed for treason in 1649 and England was declared a Commonwealth and Protectorate, a state of affairs which lasted until 1659. Although the English did not want him, Charles II was proclaimed King of the Scots in 1651. He led his army into England but they were defeated at the Battle of Worcester – a victory described by Cromwell as 'the crowning mercy'. Charles escaped and hid in an oak tree in Boscobel Wood while the Roundheads searched for him in vain. He later escaped to Bristol, dressed as a servant, and sailed away to France. It was only after Cromwell's death in 1658 that Charles was invited back to England to take the throne, and was restored to power on his thirtieth birthday, 29 May 1660.

ALFRED THE GREAT is one of the many kings linked with Winchester.

IS THIS CAMELOT? According to medieval and Tudor scholars, it was at Winchester that King Arthur held his court, although other writers say it was at Cadbury Castle in Somerset. But so strong (and so rewarding in terms of propaganda) was the cult of King Arthur during the Middle Ages that many kings and queens claimed to have descended from him. Edward I, whose bloody incursions into Wales and Scotland contrast vividly with his adoration for his first wife, Eleanor of Castile, even had a massive oak replica of King Arthur's Round Table built in about 1265. It weighs over a ton and hangs today in the Great Hall – all that is left of Winchester Castle. In the 16th century, Henry VIII ordered that the table should be decorated with a portrait of Arthur, the names of his knights and the words 'Thys is the rownde table of Kyng Arthur with xxiv of hys namyde knyghttes'.

In some respects, it is a rational assumption that the legendary king kept court here, because until the 12th century Winchester was the capital of England and an important stopping-off point on the journey to Southampton and the Continent. Before that, in the 9th century, Winchester had been created the capital of Saxon Wessex by Alfred the Great. Many kings, including Alfred, Edward the Elder and Canute, were buried at Winchester.

There have been two cathedrals at Winchester, and both are linked with notable bishops. The Saxon church, known as Hyde Abbey, was associated with St Swithin when he was Bishop of Winchester during the 9th century. When he died in 862, his funeral followed his wishes and he was buried outside the church, where the rain could fall on him. Almost a century later, the monks of Hyde Abbey decided that their saintly bishop deserved a more fitting resting place inside the church. The story goes that St Swithin's spirit was so angry at his remains being moved that he made it rain without cease for forty days until the monks put his bones back where they belonged. Ever since, weather lore states that any rain falling on St Swithin's Day (15 July) will continue for the following forty days.

Hyde Abbey was replaced with the present Norman cathedral in the 11th century. It is one of the most beautiful cathedrals in the country and, at 556 ft, is also one of the longest in Europe. Building work was carried out by a succession of bishops, the most famous being William of Wykeham who founded Winchester College in 1387. The prosperity of the see of Winchester is reflected in the ornate interior of the cathedral, with its many beautiful monuments, highly decorated choir stalls and magnificent stained glass.

The Norman kings, who so enjoyed hunting in the New Forest nearby (although William Rufus was murdered there, probably by a supporter of his younger brother Henry I), spent a lot of time at Winchester, and its celebrated position is indicated by the fact that it was excluded from the Domesday Book – London was the only other city to merit such an honour. William the Conqueror built a castle here in 1067 on the site of a previous fortress and held court in it every Easter. The royal treasury was stored here, too. Henry III was born in the castle on 1 October 1207 and later had it rebuilt. However, as the centuries wore on Winchester began to take second place to London, which had always been its rival in importance. After the English lost Normandy to the French, Winchester was no longer needed as a staging post on the journey to France and London gradually gained in supremacy, until it was officially made the capital of England in the late 12th century. The treasury and Exchequer were duly moved to Westminster. The final blow fell in 1645 when Cromwell had Winchester Castle destroyed.

Nevertheless, Winchester was still a very attractive city, and in 1683 Charles II commissioned Sir Christopher Wren to build him a magnificent palace on the site of the old castle. However, the King died long before work was completed and the plan was dropped. The buildings which had been erected were turned into a barracks and now house the regimental museum of the Royal Hussars.

THE CORONATION OF QUEEN ELIZABETH II in June 1952. She is wearing the Imperial State Crown.

AS TOURISTS JOSTLE each other to enter the imposing wooden doors of Westminster Abbey, they might spare a thought for the 11th-century king, Edward the Confessor, because he was the man responsible for building a church on this site. It was to accompany his palace, which was constructed nearby, but today there are no visible remains of his church. However, it is depicted in the Bayeux Tapestry.

Edward died in early January 1066, only a few days after the church had been consecrated. On Christmas Day of that same year – a most eventful one in English history – William the Conqueror was crowned in the church. All the Saxons who were thronged around the doorways made such a noise when shouting their approval that the Normans thought there was a riot and attacked the crowd. Several houses burnt down and many Saxons were killed in the subsequent melée.

Every medieval king lavished time and money on the church. Henry III decided to rebuild it, with the aim of making it as sumptuous as possible. He certainly achieved

his aim, and the resulting abbey borrowed many of its finest features from a number of French cathedrals.

The abbey was unfinished when Henry died yet, unlike many major English ecclesiastical buildings built piecemeal over the centuries, it has a wonderful unity of style. This is because the plans of one of Henry's original masons, Henry de Reyns, were followed as closely as possible by successive builders. The Abbot's house was also rebuilt close by, and it was in its parlour, known as the Jerusalem Chamber, that Henry IV died on 20 March 1413. It is interesting that he should have died here, because his demise fulfilled the prophesy that he would die in Jerusalem.

Although Henry VII was notorious for being mean, he continued the building of the abbey at his own expense. However, his plan to erect a shrine in the abbey to his murdered uncle, Henry VI, and have him canonized, was abandoned when the Pope named his price for the canonization process. Henry thought it far too high, so he left his uncle's body at Windsor, where it had been buried, and erected a chapel to the Virgin Mary instead.

Henry VIII dissolved the monastery that had always been part of the abbey, and although the monks returned under Mary's reign they were told to leave again once the Protestant Elizabeth I succeeded to the throne. Cromwell's army camped in the abbey during the Civil War and used the altar as an ordinary table. Cromwell was buried in the abbey but, after the Restoration, his body was exhumed, hanged at Tyburn, beheaded and buried at the foot of the gallows.

Cromwell's body may have been removed, but many other famous men and women have been buried in the abbey and their bodies allowed to stay there. In fact, there are so many tombs and memorials here that it is sometimes difficult to see the beautiful shape of the building itself, and it has now become so crowded that only ashes are accepted. Kings and queens, statesmen, soldiers, artists and writers all lie here under huge marble tombs or in ornate stone sarcophagi. It is interesting to compare the lavish designs of the royal tombs, although the very simple tomb of Edward I, which is in such marked contrast to the others, may cause a few raised eyebrows. In fact, it was deliberately kept simple so that Edward's body could be removed at any time in case of insurrection by the Scots. The plan, which he had suggested before his death, was that his corpse would be boiled to remove the flesh, and his cleaned bones taken up to Scotland where it was hoped they would have the same galvanizing effect on any Scots uprising as his living body had done. It is an idea that was never tried.

Edward I was not the only monarch whose body lay readily available in the abbey. Catherine de Valois, Queen of Henry V (whose ornate tomb and chapel are among the most important sights of the abbey), lay in an open tomb for three hundred years. She had been embalmed so successfully that, in 1669, Pepys records kissing the corpse on the mouth – it was his way of celebrating his birthday.

Some of the great names of royal history lie here – the miserly Henry VII, Anne of Cleves (the only one of Henry VIII's queens to be buried here), Edward VI, Mary Tudor, Elizabeth I, poor Mary Queen of Scots, her son James I, Charles II, Mary II, William III, Queen Anne (the last of the Stuart line) and George II. There is also the reminder of a royal mystery – one tomb holds the skeletons of two small children which were found in the Tower in 1674, during the reign of Charles II. They are believed to be the bodies of the two 'Princes in the Tower' – Edward V and his brother, Richard, Duke of York – who were probably murdered on the orders of their uncle Richard III.

Since the time of William the Conqueror, every coronation of an English sovereign has taken place here with the exception of two – Edward V, who was murdered in the Tower of London before he was crowned, and Edward VIII, who abdicated before his coronation. Some coronations went better than others. Richard II, who was overthrown by Henry IV and either murdered or starved to death, lost a shoe when he left the abbey after his coronation (something which was viewed as a bad omen at the time) and James II, who was forced to abdicate and flee to France, nearly lost his crown in the coronation procession – another ominous portent. Yet the most notorious coronation of all was that of George IV, which took place on 19 July 1821. Naturally, this flamboyant man was determined to have as lavish a ceremony as possible – it cost over £200,000 – but the excessive heat of the summer's day meant the King nearly fainted in his heavy robes and his thick make-up ran. He winked at one of the ladies during the solemn service, while outside his rejected Queen Caroline was hammering at the doors of the abbey trying to gain admittance. He had only married her so that Parliament would pay off his debts, and in the meantime she had been living in Italy 'in a most unbecoming and disgusting intimacy' with the Chamberlain of her Household. She had returned to England to take her rightful place at the coronation, and there was a public outcry over her banishment from the ceremony. To George IV's immense relief, Caroline died suddenly only a few weeks later in childbirth.

Queen Elizabeth II's coronation in the abbey was the first to be televised, although parts of the ceremony are considered so secret that they were conducted away from the cameras' prying lenses.

KING GEORGE V and Queen Mary pray at St Paul's during the Thanksgiving Jubilee Service on 6 May 1935. They had reigned for 25 years.

THE PRESENT CATHEDRAL is the fifth to stand on this site, with the first four all destroyed by fire or human hand. The fourth, built of Caen stone shipped up the Thames, was built in the 11th century, and William II (known as William Rufus), the son of William the Conqueror, contributed generously to the building costs. The cathedral became one of the largest buildings in England, much larger than the present building, and its spire was the tallest ever to have been built in the world at that time.

The old cathedral witnessed some notable royal occasions, including the lying-in-state of Richard II, and Henry V at prayer before he sailed for France in 1415. News of his subsequent victory at Agincourt was proclaimed from the cathedral steps and the king himself took part in a ceremony of thanksgiving at the cathedral a month later. Arthur, Prince of Wales, was married to Princess Catherine of Aragon here in 1501, amid much panoply. She was led up the aisle on the arm of Arthur's handsome younger brother, Prince Henry. Eight years later, following seven-and-a-half years of widowhood, Catherine married her brother-in-law, who was now King Henry VIII.

The English Reformation, in which the Church of England was established and Henry set himself up as head of that Church, was caused by his determination to rid himself of Catherine of Aragon, a wife who could not bear him a living heir. During the Reformation, St Paul's fell into such a state of disrepair that it became a short cut for people wanting to get from Carter Lane to Paternoster Row and tombs were used as shop counters. The Roman Catholic service enjoyed a brief revival there during the reign of Mary Tudor, but Protestantism returned with the succession to the throne of her half-sister, Elizabeth I.

The cathedral continued to need plenty of restoration work and by the end of the Civil War in 1660 it was in a very sorry state. Christopher Wren was commissioned to draw up plans for its restoration, but his suggestion that the whole building should be demolished and rebuilt met with scandalized refusals. As it happened, events overtook him and the Great Fire, which swept through London in the early days of September 1666, did the job of demolition for him. The only possible recourse was to remove what remained of the old St Paul's and build another cathedral in its place. Wren arranged for the building work to be carried out in stages, because he was worried by the cheese-paring attitude of the Church Commissioners. He was proved right to have been wary – in 1697 Parliament voted to halve his annual salary of £200 and he did not receive the arrears until he had successfully petitioned Queen Anne for them in 1711. Building the cathedral took 35 years, but it is a world-famous monument to a master craftsman and one of the most beautiful buildings in Britain.

Inside the cathedral, the black marble sarcophagus containing Lord Nelson's body is an interesting example of Henry VIII's acquisitive ways. The magnificent monument was originally intended for Cardinal Wolsey but, after Wolsey's disgrace, Henry took a fancy to it and appropriated it. He must have been undecided about what to do with it because it lay unused at Windsor Castle for three centuries until it was dusted off in 1806, ready for the monument in St Paul's to England's great naval hero.

Generally speaking, St Paul's has taken second place to Westminster Abbey for royal occasions, although two notable ones have taken place here within the last century. The first was the thanksgiving service attended by Queen Victoria in 1872 after her son, the Prince of Wales, recovered from typhoid – an event that effectively put paid to the republican feelings surging through the country at the time. The second was the wedding of Prince Charles to Lady Diana Spencer in July 1981. It was an occasion that showed the full splendour of St Paul's, and also emphasized the Prince's architectural interests. Since then, he has been intimately involved in the replanning of Paternoster Square, which lies to the west of the cathedral and has long been a cause for controversy.

QUEEN ELIZABETH II and Prince Philip, both wearing their insignias of the Order of the Garter, leave St Paul's after attending a special service there.

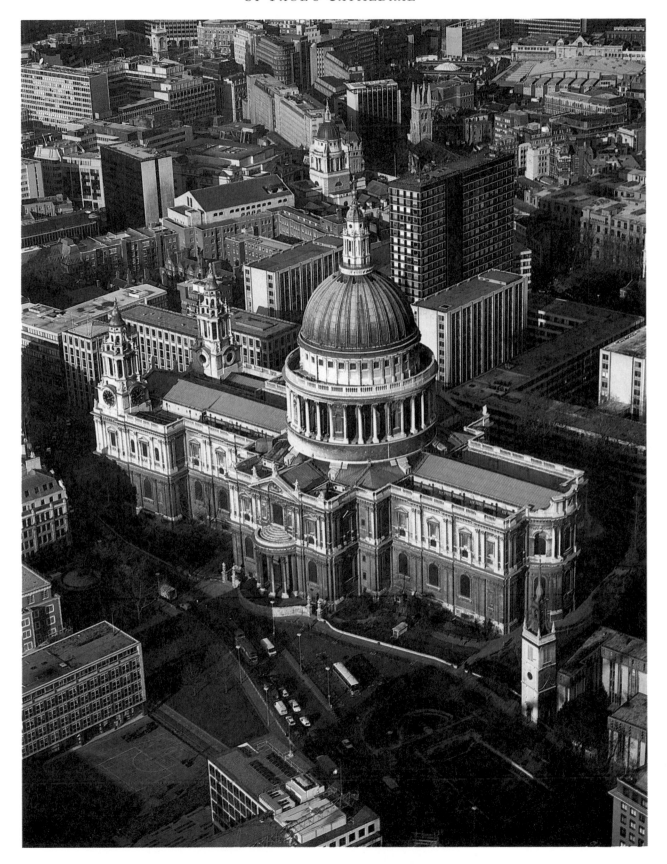

The most celebrated wedding of the 1980s took place on 29 July 1981 when Prince Charles married Lady Diana Spencer. Here, the royal family look on.

The comming of ye Kings Matte and ye Queene from Portsmouth to Hampton court.
Passage del Rey de gran Bretanha Carolo II. e o Rainha Dona Catarina de Portsmuit per a Hamton-court

THE NEWLY MARRIED CHARLES II and his Queen, Catherine of Braganza, ride in a State coach from Portsmouth to Hampton Court, which had been renovated in Catherine's honour.

IF YOU ARE LOOKING FOR ROYAL GHOSTS, try visiting Hampton Court and keep an eye out for Jane Seymour and Catherine Howard, two of Henry VIII's six wives who both met untimely ends. Jane Seymour died here after giving birth to Edward VI, and Catherine Howard was executed for treason. By a strange twist of fate, this was exactly the same punishment that had been meted out to Henry's second wife and Catherine's cousin, Anne Boleyn.

Although other kings and queens have lived here since the days of Henry VIII, he is the monarch most closely linked with the palace. Thomas Wolsey bought a 99-year lease on the site in 1514 from the Order of St John of Jerusalem, and began building. He became Cardinal and Lord Chancellor of England the following year, and Hampton Court began to assume suitably noble and sumptuous proportions. The palace was the talk of Europe, but in 1526 Wolsey presented it to Henry VIII in an effort to bolster up his fading power and placate Henry in what was generally known at the time as the 'King's Great Matter' – how he could divorce Catherine of Aragon and marry a woman who could produce an heir to the throne. In fact, this thorny problem dragged on until 1533, when Henry finally divorced himself not only from his wife but also from Rome and the Catholic Church.

Wolsey's bribe failed, his power faded completely and in 1529 his possessions – which included Hampton Court – were declared forfeit to the Crown. Henry was so delighted with the palace that it became his favourite residence and he lavished time and money on the house and gardens. Perhaps his most famous addition is the Astronomical Clock, by Nicholas Oursian, in Anne Boleyn's Gateway.

After Edward VI died, Mary Tudor spent her honeymoon here and a good part of the remaining four years of her life. Then Mary died and her successor, Elizabeth, visited Hampton Court as Queen for the first time in 1559. She must have arrived here with mixed feelings, having been kept under guard in the Water Gallery during the early part of her sister's reign. Like her father, she especially enjoyed working in the gardens, and her splendid Elizabethan court conducted itself with great pomp and ceremony here. Hampton Court was especially festive under the rule of Elizabeth, a tradition which her successor, James I, was determined to continue. His son, Charles I, had a less happy time at the palace because, as well

as annoying the neighbours by digging up their land to install some water features in his own, he spent much of his time seeking refuge here during the run-up to the Civil War. He was imprisoned here after the war and, following his execution, Hampton Court was put up for sale by the new Parliament. The proceeds were to be used to cover the royal debts but Oliver Cromwell stopped the sale and moved in with his family.

Charles II became the new owner after the Restoration, and he had his work cut out for him making good all the damage that had been done to the palace during the Civil War. By the time William and Mary moved into the palace in 1688, the apartments were considered old-fashioned and Sir Christopher Wren was commissioned to produce a building more in keeping with the new age. The combination of Mary's early death and a severe lack of money put paid to Wren's original plan of demolishing virtually all the palace and building 'a new Versailles' in its place. Yet even though Wren's plans were curtailed, the renovations were not completed until 1699, three years before William's death. This was caused partly by a fall from his horse at Hampton Court, when it stumbled over a molehill. Queen Anne inherited the debts that William had accrued as well as the building that had caused them, but her ill health meant she could not enjoy Hampton Court in the way she had hoped. George I looked on the place as a refuge from the strange country he found himself in, and his son, George II, entertained his friends here to many high jinks whenever his father was away. Yet he was the last English monarch to live here.

Among the great names to stamp their genius on the palace were Verrio (who painted the King's Staircase, featuring the faces of all the parlour maids he slept with during his stay), Capability Brown, Sir John Vanbrugh, Lely and Kneller. George III began the tradition of letting out parts of the palace as 'grace and favour' apartments – a practice which is still continued to this day.

If you visit Hampton Court today it is like having a crash course in history. The buildings are immaculately preserved and if it were not for the throng of fellow visitors you might easily imagine you had stepped back into the past, especially if it is a beautifully sunny day and you have arrived by boat from Westminster or Richmond – the favourite means of transport here of such previous inhabitants as Henry VIII.

THE OFFICIAL LONDON RESIDENCE of the Queen, Buckingham Palace acts like a magnet for many tourists. Selected rooms are now being opened to the public, whereas before the only way most people entered these hallowed portals was by invitation.

George IV commissioned the palace, having declared that Carlton House, until then the London residence of the royal family, was no longer grand enough and should be demolished. This must have been black news indeed to government ministers who had already watched an extravagant George III spend the previous thirty years renovating Carlton House at what the King himself called 'enormous' expense. Sure enough, history began to repeat itself at Buckingham Palace, because George IV insisted on making his new home so splendid that it finally cost the State £700,000 – a staggering sum by contemporary standards and twice what the Prime Minister had said was his upper limit. John Nash was the architect and may well have found the royal commission to be a poisoned chalice – he was constantly being questioned about the spiralling costs and his designs were soundly criticized. To make matters worse, Nash proposed that parts of the palace which had already been built but had met with the King's disapproval should be pulled down and rebuilt. Wellington, by then Prime Minister, gave him a very dusty answer but the work went ahead all the same. George IV and his successor, William IV, were both dead by the time the place was habitable and Queen Victoria was the first monarch to live here.

By this time, Nash had been given his marching orders and Edward Blore commissioned to take over and complete the project. He added the east front – the part of the palace best known to tourists today – which involved removing Marble Arch, which had stood there, to its present position at the top of Park Lane. Queen Victoria liked the palace, which is interesting because she loathed that other symbol of Georgian extravagance, Brighton Pavilion. It was at Buckingham Palace that her son Edward VII was born and where George V brought up his children. Although Edward VIII, later the Duke of Windsor, disliked it, his brother, George VI, was happy here.

Since the widespread intrusion of the photographic and television cameras into the lives of the royal family, Buckingham Palace has become a focal point for State occasions. The photographs taken here on VE day, 8 May 1945, are among the most vivid images of London's role in the Second World War. They show George VI, Queen Elizabeth and the Princesses Elizabeth and Margaret, accompanied by Sir Winston Churchill, standing on the famous balcony at the palace in front of boarded-up windows, waving at a sea of faces thronging back up the Mall. Equally memorable are the photographs of the King and Queen picking their way through the wreckage when the palace was bombed in September 1940. 'I'm glad we've been bombed,' the Queen said. 'It makes me feel I can look the East End in the face.' Her husband was not so sanguine, believing that the chapel had been 'wrecked'.

More recently the palace balcony has been the traditional place for the royal family to wave at the crowds on wedding days. National euphoria reached new heights on 29 July 1981 when Prince Charles married Lady Diana Spencer and the couple broke all royal traditions by exchanging a heartfelt kiss in front of the watching world.

THE DIAMOND JUBILEE year of King George V was 1935. He is shown here attending a garden party at Buckingham Palace with Queen Mary (nearest the camera) and other members of the royal family. The King died in the following January.

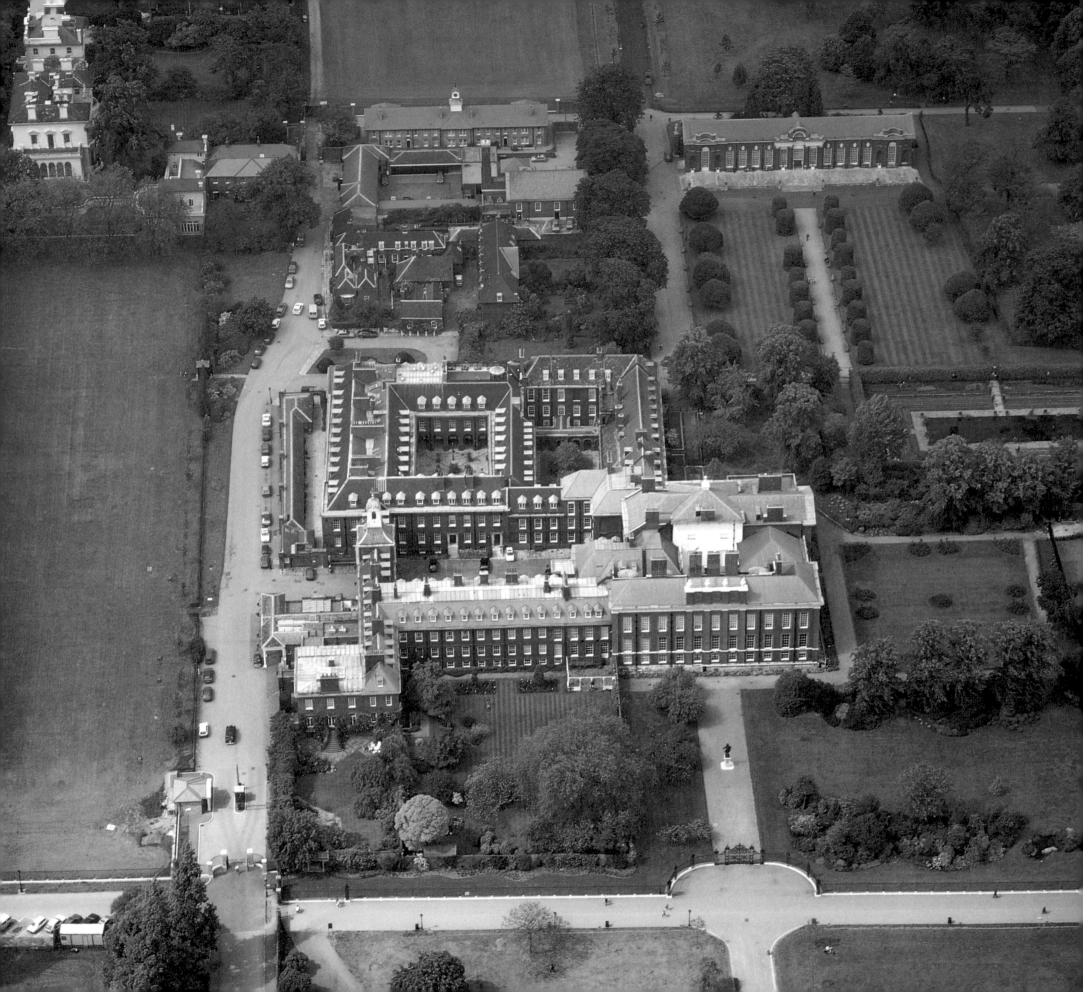

PRINCESS MAY (later Queen Mary) with her mother, the Duchess of Teck, at Kensington Palace, on the engagement of Princess May to George, Duke of York (later George V), in 1893.

KENSINGTON PALACE was originally known as Nottingham House because it belonged to William III's Secretary of State, the Earl of Nottingham. It was bought for William and Mary, his Queen, in 1689. Whitehall Palace, where they lived at the time, was deemed too damp for the King's asthma, so they moved to Hampton Court while renovation work was carried out on Nottingham House. Sir Christopher Wren was the architect and Nicholas Hawksmoor was Clerk of the Works, but Mary was so impatient to move in that short cuts were made by the builders and, in November 1689, some of the new buildings 'being newly covered with lead, fell down in a sudden and hurt several people, and killed some'.

The royal family had moved in by Christmas of the same year, although the palace was barely in a fit state, and much of the hard work that had been carried out was destroyed by a fire in November 1691. When William died in 1702 Queen Anne moved in and changed the layout of the gardens. She died here, after a succession of illnesses, on 1 August 1714. Her doctor commented 'I believe sleep was never more welcome to a weary traveller than death was to her.' She left Kensington Palace in a state of considerable disrepair, but her successor, George I, liked it because it reminded him of his home in Hanover. It was he who brought in William Kent, who transformed the State Apartments and painted a magnificent *trompe-l'oeuil* up the King's Staircase, showing people leaning over balustrades to watch the comings and goings of the King's courtiers. George II and his wife, Queen Caroline, made further changes, including the building of the Round Pond and the Broad Walk, both of which are now part of Kensington Gardens.

After the death of George II, Kensington Palace fell into disrepair once more, because the late King's grandson, George III, preferred to live at Buckingham House. Nevertheless, he allocated a set of rooms to his fourth son, the Duke of Kent, but he was obliged to go abroad to escape his debts and various other members of the vast royal family lived there instead. In 1819 the Duke of Kent returned to Kensington Palace with his new and pregnant wife, Princess Victoria of Saxe-Coburg-Saalfeld, so she could give birth to their child in England. He had taken part in a race with his brothers to see who could produce the next heir to the British throne, and he won. His daughter was born in the Palace on 24 May of the same year, and christened Victoria. It was in Kensington Palace in the early hours of 20 June 1837 that the young Victoria was roused from sleep by the Archbishop of Canterbury and the Lord Chamberlain and told she had just become Queen of England. She was to reign for over sixty years.

Princess May of Teck, who married George V and became Queen Mary, was also born at Kensington Palace and lived here in her youth with her recklessly extravagant parents. When she was in her teens Queen Victoria sent her and her parents to Florence because her mother had run up debts of nearly £70,000 and the bailiffs were about to call.

Today, parts of Kensington Palace are open to the public, including the State Apartments and William Kent's wonderful King's staircase, while others have been divided up into grace and favour apartments. Many members of the immediate royal family have apartments here.

PRINCESS CAROLINE OF BRUNSWICK lands at Greenwich on
5 April 1795.

IN THE MIDDLE AGES, Greenwich Palace was a favourite residence of the Tudor monarchs. It was placed conveniently by the Thames and was not far from the Tower of London and the Palace of Westminster, so was easily accessible by boat. Greenwich Palace was also claimed to be one of the finest houses in England, although none of it remains today.

The palace came into royal hands in 1445 when the Duke of Gloucester, who had built it, lent it to Henry VI and his wife, Margaret of Anjou, for their honeymoon. Henry liked it so much that, two years later when Gloucester was arrested and died, he decided to live here himself. Subsequent kings and queens lived here, and Henry VIII was born in the palace on 28 June 1491. He loved it, because he could hunt in the extensive grounds (now Greenwich Park) and watch the busy traffic on the Thames. He also extended the palace, adding armouries and a banqueting hall. Both his daughters were born here – Mary on 8 February 1516 and, a good many years later, Elizabeth on 7 September 1533.

It was at Greenwich that an impatient Henry waited for the arrival of his new bride in the winter of 1539. He had not met Anne of Cleves, but the Holbein portrait he had been sent was very promising. Another consideration in his new wife's favour was that, politically, it was a very good marriage. However, when Henry finally met Anne at Rochester Castle all he felt was disappointment. 'I like her not' he told Cromwell, who had been the chief instigator of the match. Nevertheless, the wedding went ahead on 6 January 1540, and took place in the Queen's Closet at Greenwich. The following morning, Cromwell asked the King how his wedding night had gone – 'How liked you the Queen?' A bitter Henry replied 'I liked her before not well, but now I like her much worse.' He later claimed that she had been so unattractive he was unable to make love to her, and the marriage was never consummated. In Anne's defence, it must be said that Henry was experiencing periodic bouts of impotence, but naturally he was quick to lay the blame on his new bedfellow. Henry still wanted an heir, but knew that Anne of Cleves was not the woman to bear him one and she never got the chance to do so. Six months later they were divorced and, on 28 July of the same year, Henry married Catherine Howard.

Edward VI was sent to Greenwich in April 1553 for the sake of his failing health, but he died here from tuberculosis on 6 July 1553. His successor and half-sister, Mary, rarely visited Greenwich, perhaps because her mother, Catherine of Aragon, had had miserable memories of the place. One occasion when Mary did visit cannot have been encouraging – a cannon was fired to salute her presence and the cannon ball tore through the walls of her apartment, narrowly missing her. Was she that unpopular? Her half-sister, Elizabeth I, came to Greenwich each summer, and it is here that Sir Walter Raleigh laid his cloak over a puddle to protect her feet.

During the Civil War the palace was put up for sale but there were no takers and so it was turned into a factory instead. After the Restoration, Charles II decided to rebuild the palace but the work was never completed and eventually the building was demolished, and the Royal Naval Hospital was built in its place.

Another palace was built in the grounds of Greenwich Park in the 17th century, designed by Inigo Jones, and was known as the Queen's House. It was originally intended for the wife of James I, Anne of Denmark, but she died before it was completed. Queen Henrietta Maria, wife of Charles I, enjoyed the house so much that she called it the 'House of Delights'. During the Civil War the house was kept by the Parliamentarians and became the place where Commonwealth generals were laid in state before their funerals. Following the Restoration, Queen Henrietta Maria continued to live here, and after her death the house belonged to Catherine of Braganza (Queen of Charles II) and then Mary of Modena (Queen of James II). William III and Mary II did not use the house because it was too near the river, and therefore bad for William's weak chest. George I held his first official reception here, in 1714, after his arrival from Hanover. He had inherited the throne through his mother, Sophia, a Protestant grand-daughter of James I, after Queen Anne had died without leaving an heir.

By 1806 the Queen's House had become a school for the orphans of sailors, and remained so until 1933 when the school moved to Suffolk. The house began a new life in 1937 as the central part of the National Maritime Museum, and is still used as such today.

ALTHOUGH MOST PEOPLE call this building the Houses of Parliament, it is a royal palace and has been so since the first palace was built by Edward the Confessor. The Palace of Westminster was the main residence of all English kings and the centre of Court life until the reign of Henry VIII, who preferred Whitehall Palace because he found Westminster too draughty. He also liked to be away from his Queen, Catherine of Aragon, so he could enjoy himself with her lady-in-waiting, Anne Boleyn.

Originally, the King's Council had met in Westminster Hall, built by William Rufus, but in the early 14th century the system of having Commons and Lords was introduced and they met separately in the palace. The Lords were allowed to use the White Chamber but the Commons had to find an empty room and sometimes met in the refectory. During the reign of Henry VIII, the Commons found a new home in the magnificent St Stephen's Chapel, and it remained the House of Commons until it was destroyed by fire in 1834. Luckily the crypt, which formed the lower storey of the chapel, survived and is today used as a chapel by Members of both Houses.

The fire of 1834 destroyed most of the original Palace of Westminster, succeeding where a gang of Roman Catholic conspirators had failed in 1605. This was the Gunpowder Plot, when Guido Fawkes and his friends were caught on 5 November trying to blow up James I and the Houses of Parliament. They hoped that if they killed the King and most of Parliament they would be able to take over the country and ensure religious tolerance of their outlawed faith. They rented a cellar underneath the Queen's Chamber, which was the meeting place of the House of Lords, and filled it with barrels of gunpowder. However, a tip-off led to their discovery and they either died while resisting arrest or were executed and their severed heads stuck on spikes. Before each State Opening of Parliament, the cellars where the gunpowder was hidden are still ceremonially searched to ensure history is not repeated.

Another tradition of the Palace of Westminster is that no monarch can enter the Commons Chamber – during the State Opening of Parliament the reigning monarch sits on the throne in the House of Lords. This dates back to the unhappy reign of Charles I, when he rushed into St Stephen's Chapel in January 1642 to demand that five dissident MPs, who were absent at the time, should be arrested. When Charles asked where they were, the Speaker replied 'I have neither eyes to see, nor tongue to speak in this place, but as this House is pleased to direct me.' Charles was given no option but to leave. It was the start of the Civil War and the end of Charles' reign.

The fire of 1834 swept through the Palace of Westminster and destroyed virtually all of it, providing a marvellous opportunity to design a new building specifically to house Parliament. Charles Barry and Augustus Pugin were commissioned to carry out the work, and Prince Albert oversaw the project. During the Blitz of the Second World War, the Houses of Parliament were damaged eleven times, culminating in an almighty fire on the night of 10 May 1941. The House of Commons and Lobby were reduced to ash, and were rebuilt in the style of the old chamber by Sir Giles Gilbert Scott.

CHARLES I WAS EXECUTED outside the Banqueting Hall on 30 January 1649 in front of a horrified crowd.

ONLY THE BANQUETING HOUSE, designed by Inigo Jones, remains of Whitehall Palace which was the chief London residence of the Court during the reign of Henry VIII. Today it stands on Whitehall, in front of the Ministry of Defence (see opposite, top left).

The palace had originally belonged to the See of York, at which time it was called York Place. It was the official London residence of the Archbishop of York and the then incumbent of that office, Thomas Wolsey, lived there from 1514-1529, when his popularity went into a sudden and dramatic decline after he failed to procure Henry VIII's divorce from Catherine of Aragon. Henry had always enjoyed visiting York Place so he moved in, because it was much more comfortable and fashionable than the Palace of Westminster. It also lacked special apartments for Queen Catherine, so Henry was able to spend time here with Anne Boleyn, whom he wanted to marry. The house was renamed Whitehall Palace and Henry married Anne and, later, Jane Seymour, here.

During the reign of James I it was decided to rebuild the palace completely, but only the Banqueting House was built. It was to have a fatal significance for James' son, Charles I.

Charles I's autocratic belief in the divine right of kings was a central part of his Stuart inheritance but it eventually cost him his life. A series of mismanaged wars led Parliament to withdraw the funds for any more costly débâcles, so Charles dissolved it. He reigned without any Parliament at all from 1629-1640, only reconvening it in the hope of being awarded money to finance another disastrous war, this time against his own subjects in Scotland. By this time Parliament was deeply suspicious of the King, a situation not helped by the taxes that had been levied by the King's Government during the long interval between Parliaments. Parliament demanded that one of Charles' advisors should be arrested and executed for treason without going to trial, and over the next two years the many grievances between King and Parliament polarized into two sides – the Royalists and the Parliamentarians. Both factions were anxious to avert a civil war so negotiations were conducted for seven months, but they broke down when Parliament demanded too many compromises from the King.

The first Civil War started in Nottingham on 22 August 1642 but Charles's vacillations and empty promises to the English, Scots, Irish and Puritans meant that all trust in him gradually melted away. Finally, in 1647 he was caught by the Roundheads, led by Thomas Fairfax and Oliver Cromwell. Charles was imprisoned in Hampton Court but escaped and made his way to the Isle of Wight, where he played off his enemies against each other. A second Civil War broke out in 1648 but was quickly over, and Charles was charged with waging war on his own people. He was taken to Westminster Hall in January 1649 to face trial, but he declared the court was illegal and did not bother to defend himself. However, he had already been condemned and probably could not have saved himself whatever he said. He was condemned to death and executed in full view of the watching crowds on 30 January 1649, on a scaffold erected outside the Banqueting House. It was a bitterly cold morning and the deposed King wore two shirts to keep warm – he was worried that if he shivered in the low temperature it would be mistaken for terror.

Cromwell lived in the palace during the Commonwealth and died here in 1658. After the Restoration, Charles II lived here in a *menage à quatre* with his wife and two of his mistresses and died in the palace on 6 February 1685. His brother and successor, James II, built a Roman Catholic chapel in the palace and, when his pro-Catholic views lost him the throne and made him fear for his life, it was from Whitehall that he escaped on 11 December 1688. Whether by accident or design, he dropped the Great Seal of England in the Thames at Westminster as he fled. It has never been found.

William III and Mary II, who had overthrown him, did not like Whitehall Palace because its proximity to the river was bad for William's asthma, so after being proclaimed King and Queen here they transferred their official London residence to Kensington Palace. In 1698 Whitehall Palace was burned to the ground after a Dutch laundress forgot about the clothes she was drying before a fire. The resulting conflagration destroyed everything but the Banqueting House, which still stands and can be visited by the public.

WHEN JOHN VANBRUGH began planning the lavish Blenheim Palace in 1705, comfort and the creation of a happy homely atmosphere were hardly considerations. Instead, he wanted to create a monument to the Duke of Marlborough, one of Britain's greatest soldiers and the victor of the Battle of Blenheim, which had been waged in Bavaria the previous year by the English and the Austrians against the French and Bavarian forces.

Queen Anne granted the land, which comprised the Royal Manor of Woodstock, and also forwarded the money to build this fitting tribute to a great soldier. John Vanbrugh was commissioned to begin work and among his helpers was Nicholas Hawksmoor. However, it was not an easy time for him because he was hampered at every turn by the temperamental Duchess of Marlborough, who had wanted Sir Christopher Wren to work on the house and made her dissatisfaction very plain. Sarah, the Duchess, had been the great friend of Queen Anne but she managed to fall out with her between 1708 and 1709, partly because of her haughty attitude towards Anne and partly because of Anne's friendship with a lady-in-waiting. Sarah was Mistress of the Robes, having first served the Queen when she was the Princess Anne, and the many years of friendship between the two women meant that Sarah believed she could speak her mind. She was a Whig and the newly favoured lady-in-waiting a Tory, and Sarah's continual outbursts and naggings eventually eroded the friendship between herself and the Queen — and ensured that Anne became a faithful Tory. The affair ended with Sarah's dismissal in 1711 and the Duke was forced to live abroad until Anne died in 1714.

Work continued on Blenheim Palace in the meantime. The Duke had a stroke in 1716 and all control of the building passed to his Duchess, at which point Vanbrugh, unable to face any more rows and upsets, resigned. All the State money had long since dried up, and the

Marlboroughs were left footing the bill for the remaining work – it cost them £50,000. Queen Anne's gardener, Henry Wise, originally laid out the grounds and Capability Brown finished them in 1784.

Another great statesman linked with Blenheim is Sir Winston Churchill who was born here on 30 November 1874. Until the 9th Duke had a son, Churchill was heir presumptive to Blenheim and was a frequent visitor to the palace throughout his life. Incidentally, although it is called a palace, it is the only non-royal palace in Britain.

At the time of writing, another fierce and bitter argument is raging at Blenheim. This time it is being waged between the present Duke of Marlborough and his son, Jamie Blandford, over whether or not he will inherit the palace. However, visitors to Blenheim can ignore such headline-grabbing topics and simply revel in the beauties that are on offer in the house and grounds. The view of the lake and the house was once described by Lord Randolph Churchill as 'the finest in England', and the 2200 acres of parkland (which include two apparently natural lakes, created by Capability Brown after he dammed the River Glyme) roll splendidly in all directions. Inside the house, there are magnificent painted ceilings and sumptuous State rooms, all of which are full of reminders of Marlborough's triumphant military career. The banqueting hall is an example, with the Duke's coat of arms painted above each vast marble doorway, and the painted ceiling depicting Marlborough riding through heaven in a chariot. On the walls are painted columns and a host of spectators, some of whom are chatting to one another while others gaze down on the long dining table below them. It is obvious that money was no object when Blenheim was built, and equally clear that the building costs vastly exceeded even the most generous estimate. Today that is something for which to be thankful, because without doubt Blenheim is one of the nation's greatest treasures.

Visitors to eltham today may find it hard to believe that this was once the site of a royal palace, yet the evidence is there for all to see. The building is now leased to the Institute of Education, but the Great Hall – one of three important great halls which still survive – is open to the public. The other two great halls are at Westminster and Hampton Court.

Eltham passed into royal hands in the early 14th century, when it was given to Edward, Prince of Wales, by the then owner, Anthony Bek, Bishop of Durham. In due course, Edward became Edward II, and he gave Eltham to his Queen, Isabella. It was handed down from father to son, and during the reign of Richard II a lot of improvements were made to the palace, under the supervision of one Geoffrey Chaucer, clerk of the works. When Chaucer was not busy at Eltham he was writing his poems, including, of course, *The Canterbury Tales*.

In 1445, Henry VI ordered a spate of new building 'in all haste possible' ready for the arrival of his new wife, Margaret of Anjou. He must have known that time was not on his side, and that Fate was not either – his cousin Richard, Duke of York, was casting covetous eyes over the throne. Henry's unhappy reign was notable not only because he was crowned three times (at Westminster Abbey in 1429, in Paris in 1431 and in St Paul's Cathedral in 1470) but because he was twice deposed from the throne and died in the Tower of London. He also had to contend with periodic bouts of insanity and the Wars of the Roses.

This civil war, which lasted for thirty years, was waged between the rival houses of Lancaster and York. Margaret of Anjou, Henry's Queen, was the leader of the Lancastrians and the Duke of York was the leader of the rival Yorkists. Both Henry and the Duke of York wanted the throne, and both had descended from Edward III. Henry became no more than a pawn in the bids for the throne, and was seized by the Yorkists in 1460. He was recaptured but the Duke of York declared himself heir to the throne in October. He was killed in battle on the last day of the year but his son, Edward, took up the cause. Henry was deposed and Edward IV was declared King by Parliament on 4 March 1461. Until now the Yorkist cause had been espoused by the powerful Richard Neville, known as Warwick the Kingmaker, but in the late 1460s Warwick's allegiance changed and he drove Edward IV into exile, restoring Henry to the throne on 3 October 1470. Warwick ruled on Henry's behalf.

Such a state of affairs did not last long. On Easter Sunday, 14 April 1471, the Lancastrians were routed in the Battle of Barnet and Warwick was killed. The Battle of Tewkesbury followed on 4 May, and ended the Lancastrian cause. Margaret of Anjou was captured and imprisoned, and Henry VI was sent back to the Tower of London, where it was said he died 'of pure displeasure and melancholy' on 21 May 1471. The unofficial version of his death is that he was murdered while saying his prayers.

Yet the Lancastrians had not been defeated. Although Henry's son, Edward, was murdered in 1471, the exiled heir to the Lancastrians, Henry Tudor, was waiting in the wings. The Yorkist Richard III was on the throne but his power was slipping fast, and on 22 August 1485 his reign ended when he was killed by Henry Tudor at the Battle of Bosworth. It was the effective end of the Wars of the Roses and the beginning of the great Tudor dynasty.

Henry VIII was the last monarch to visit Eltham regularly, and his daughter Elizabeth I was an even more infrequent visitor because she much preferred the nearby palace at Greenwich. Parliament took possession of Eltham after Charles I was beheaded and the palace began to fall into rack and ruin. The Great Hall, which had been used as a barn during the intervening centuries, was restored in the 1930s and a new house was built.

SCONE (which is pronounced *skoon*, incidentally, and has nothing to do with the floury cake of the same name) stands right at the heart of Scotland, just north of Perth. It was once the capital of Pictland, the home of the northern Picts (which means 'painted people', referring to the tattoos with which they decorated themselves), at the time when Scotland was divided into four tribal kingdoms – Dalriada (comprising part of Northern Ireland, the Inner Hebrides and Argyll), the Kingdom of the Britons (Strathclyde), the Kingdom of the Angles (south-east Scotland) and Pictland (northern Scotland). Scotland eventually became united under the kings of Dalriada, and so all Scots kings followed the same path of being crowned at Scone Abbey and, when their time came, buried on Iona (which was also a part of Dalriada). The first recorded Scottish Parliament convened at Scone in AD 906.

Alexander I founded an abbey here in 1115, and a palace was soon built to accompany it. Scone also housed an object which was considered sacred to Scotland – the Stone of Destiny, upon which all Scots kings were crowned. It is believed to have come originally from Tara in Ireland, and to be Lower Old Red Sandstone. Kenneth MacAlpin is reputed to have moved the precious stone to a monastery here from its previous home at Dunstaffnage Castle on Loch Etive because he considered it to be in jeopardy where it was. Little did he realize that it would be seized by Edward I in 1296 and carried down to Westminster Abbey, along with other national treasures such as the holy rood of Queen (St) Margaret. This was a typical example of Edward's belligerent attitude towards Scotland and Wales, which he had also stripped of its treasures, and to say that it was not appreciated would be a gross understatement. Such actions provoked the prolonged and bloody Scottish War of Independence which was still being fought long after he died in 1307. It was his grandson, the young Edward III, who brought

the fighting to an end in 1328, when he surrendered to the Scots. He agreed to return all Scotland's most precious documents and prized objects, including the holy rood, but curiously the Stone of Destiny was not mentioned and remained in Westminster Abbey, where it can still be seen today, under the Coronation Chair.

Stone of Destiny or not, Scots kings continued to be crowned at Scone Abbey, with the infant James II of Scotland being the exception – he was crowned at Holyrood. The last coronation to take place at Scone was on 1 January 1651, when Charles II was proclaimed King of the Scots. He had been proclaimed King of England in 1649, but remained uncrowned and powerless while England continued to be in the grip of the Commonwealth under Oliver Cromwell. After his Scottish coronation he invaded England, but it was not a successful manoeuvre and he fled to France after losing the Battle of Worcester in 1651. His restoration finally came in 1660.

In the meantime, the original abbey and palace at Scone had both been burnt down in 1559, and the land was given to the Ruthvens – a family who were to play a notorious part in Scottish history. After their attempt to murder the young James VI of Scotland in 1600 during the Gowrie conspiracy, the land was passed to Sir David Murray of Gospertie and it has remained in his family ever since. He completed the palace which had been begun by the Earl of Gowrie, but the present palace was built in the early 1800s by the 3rd Earl of Mansfield. It is made of red sandstone and was designed by William Atkinson, a pupil of James Wyatt, in Gothic style. It is open to the public and houses a superb collection of china, ivories and French furniture, including a writing table made for Marie Antoinette. The palace also contains bed-hangings embroidered by Mary Queen of Scots and her ladies.

REGENT MORAY ruled on behalf of his nephew, James VI of Scotland, but was murdered at Linlithgow on 23 January 1570.

ONCE THE PRINCIPAL ROYAL RESIDENCE of Scottish kings, from James I to James VI, Linlithgow is now a ruin. Even so, it is remarkably well preserved – fittingly so, considering that so much Scottish royal history was acted out within its walls.

A royal manor was built at Linlithgow in 1139, during the reign of David I, but it was quite simple and unpretentious. Edward I arrived from England in 1301 and commissioned James of St George to build a fort here. The architect had built Edward's Welsh castles, but his stonemasons were not anxious to repeat the experience of working for Edward after they had finished Linlithgow – he was reluctant to pay them and they said they would rather go into exile than work for him again. Sadly, all their hard (and unrewarded) work was demolished in 1314 after the Scots victory at Bannockburn, when all English fortifications in Scotland were razed to the ground. The son of Robert the Bruce, who had routed Edward II at Bannockburn, had another royal manor built here, but it was burnt down in 1424.

Most of Linlithgow, as it stands today, was built by James I who often came to the palace during its construction to see what was happening. Successive kings continued his work, although James IV is most closely connected with the palace and he was still rebuilding Linlithgow in 1513 when he was killed at Flodden. Tradition has it that his wife, Queen Margaret, sat forlornly in a little chamber at the top of the north-west tower, now known as Queen Margaret's Bower, awaiting his return from Flodden. She waited in vain, and instead of seeing her triumphant husband return home from the wars, she saw a horseman arriving with some very bad news.

The grand-daughter of James IV and Margaret, Mary Queen of Scots, was born here on 7 December 1542. Her father, James V, did not live to see her and died at Falkland Palace six days after her birth, broken-hearted after the Scots were routed by the English at Solway Moss on 24 November. James was equally miserable at the news that his new child was a girl. His two baby sons had died the previous year, and he had longed for another son who would be heir to the Scottish throne. When he heard that he had a daughter, he apparently said 'Adieu, fare well, it came with a lass, it will pass with a lass.' This remark referred to the marriage of Marjorie Bruce to Walter the Steward which had founded the Stuart dynasty. History would prove him right, but the Stuart line did not die with Mary Queen of Scots – it ended in 1714 with the death of Queen Anne who, despite having had seventeen pregnancies, died without a direct heir. Two other Stewarts, James 'The Old Pretender' and his son Charles 'The Young Pretender' asserted their rights to the throne in 1715 and 1745 respectively, but both failed in the attempt.

Mary's son, James VI of Scotland and later James I of England, carried out restoration work on Linlithgow between 1618 and 1620 but the building was nearing the end of its life as a royal palace. The luckless Charles I came here in 1633 and such was the panoply that surrounded his visit that all the turf roofs on houses near the palace were replaced with slates specially for the occasion. However, new slate roofs did not stop him being beheaded and, in a sinister omen suited to his fate, all the royal swans were said to have left Linlithgow when he departed. Apparently they only returned after the Restoration.

Bonnie Prince Charlie, 'The Young Pretender', visited Linlithgow on 15 September 1745 on his way from Stirling to Edinburgh, where he made a triumphant entry into the city. But it was his campaign which brought about Linlithgow's downfall because, the following year, English soldiers camped in the palace and lit fires to keep themselves warm. When they left, they did not trouble to stamp out these fires and the resulting conflagration robbed Linlithgow of its roof and reduced it to its present state.

HOLYROODHOUSE is the Queen's official residence in Scotland, and it is perfectly situated at one end of the Royal Mile, with Edinburgh Castle standing at the other. The palace and abbey that make up Holyroodhouse stand beneath the brooding basaltic bulk of Salisbury Crags and Arthur's Seat, which is an extinct volcano.

The list of kings and queens connected with Holyroodhouse is endless, and the name itself comes from the bequest of one of them, the 11th-century Queen Margaret. She was the second wife of Malcolm III, who killed Macbeth in 1057 and assumed the Scottish throne the following year. Queen Margaret (now known to the Scots as St Margaret) left her precious relic of Christ's cross, called the 'holy rood', to her son, David. When he became David I the Saint, he built an abbey here in 1128 to house the relic, and called it Holyrood Abbey. For centuries, until the Reformation, this was the burial place of numerous kings and queens, many of whom were also born and married here. The abbey is in ruins today, partly due to various pillagings over the years and partly because of the new roof it was given in the 16th century. This roof proved to be too heavy, and collapsed on the abbey in 1768.

The building of the remarkably beautiful palace began in 1498 under James IV, an inspired king who made the city of Edinburgh famous throughout the world as a seat of learning. He began developing the guesthouse which was attached to the abbey but his building work was never completed – it was ended by his death at Flodden. Much of the present palace was built by Charles II after the Restoration, between 1671 and 1680. His master mason, Robert Mylne, carried out most of the work under the supervision of Sir William Bruce.

Yet the monarch most closely associated with the palace is Mary Queen of Scots who spent six years of her reign here, from 1561 to 1567, long before Charles II was born. She lived in the tower built by James IV, and it was here that one of the most notorious Scottish murders took place. Mary became Queen of Scotland on 14 December 1542, when she was only seven days old, after the death of her father, James V – a fitting start for someone whose life would be peppered with plots, counter-plots, imprisonments and murders.

The first plot against her took place in July 1543 when Henry VIII attempted to betroth her to his son and only heir, Prince Edward, but this was rightly seen as a ruse on Henry's part to gain control of the Scottish throne and was denounced by the Scots at the end of that year. Henry punished Scotland by sending invasions of bloodthirsty English troops, a time known as the 'Rough Wooing', and the country quickly re-established its 'Auld Alliance' with France. In fact, Mary was believed to be the living embodiment of this, with her Scottish father and French mother, and she grew up in France under the care of her mother's Roman Catholic family. In 1558, at the age of sixteen, Mary married the Dauphin, who later became Francis II, and Elizabeth I succeeded to the English throne. This succession was seen by all European Roman Catholics as wrong, because in their eyes Elizabeth was illegitimate and Mary was the rightful queen of England. Civil war broke out in Scotland as a result, with the Protestant John Knox thundering against Mary's mother, the Catholic Mary of Guise. But the French had no efficient representatives in Scotland and the Protestants gained the upper hand, suppressing Catholicism in Scotland. Francis II died in December 1560 and Mary returned to Scotland in April of the following year to reign as its Queen. In the meantime, both English and Scottish statesmen were debating who should be Mary's second husband. She eventually married her first cousin, Henry Stewart (Stuart), Lord Darnley. His mother was second in line to the English throne after Mary herself, and it was a marriage that strengthened Mary's claims to the English succession. They were married in Holyrood Chapel on 29 July 1565. Darnley was declared King Henry but already his vain and swaggering nature was making him highly unpopular. As time went on he became greedy for more power and his father wanted him to be given the crown matrimonial, which would ensure independent royal status. This was meat and drink to Mary's enemies, but they had reckoned without Darnley's own actions. Although Mary was pregnant with the future James VI of Scotland, relations were strained between husband and wife and Mary's friend and secretary, David Riccio, whom it was whispered was her lover, had advised her not to concede to Darnley's wishes. A furious Darnley, together with the Earl of Morton, plotted to kill Riccio in revenge.

On the night of 9 March 1566 Darnley, with a posse of collaborators – which included the notorious Patrick Lord Ruthven, generally presumed to be a warlock and a man whose son and grandson would both figure prominently in the life of Mary's unborn child – climbed the private staircase that led to the Queen's apartments and interrupted a supper party that she was holding. Riccio, who was a small man, clung to the pregnant Queen's skirts but was dragged off and stabbed, some sixty times, using Darnley's own dagger. His body was dragged down the main staircase and dumped on a chest, then later buried in the grounds of Holyrood. Although Mary had been convinced that her life was in danger too from her husband, who wanted to rule Scotland by himself, she persuaded him to escape with her to Dunbar Castle to get away from his accomplices. They returned to Edinburgh on 28 March, riding back in triumph and guarded by 2000 horsemen under the command of the faithful Bothwell, who was one of her courtiers and had escaped on the night of Riccio's murder by jumping out of a window at Holyrood. He had believed, with good reason, that he would be murdered too.

The following year, Darnley, who was convalescing from an attack of syphillis at a house called Kirk o' Field (long since vanished but somewhere near the present university in South Bridge Street), was murdered. The house was blown up in the night and Darnley's strangled body was found lying in the garden the following morning. Bothwell was accused of his murder (rightly so, it is generally believed) and acquitted, and then set about ensuring he would marry the newly widowed queen. He did just that, in Holyrood Chapel, on 15 May 1567 – only two months after Darnley's death. Bothwell was a Protestant and outraged Scottish lords decided they had had enough of this. Mary was imprisoned at Lochleven and forced to abdicate in favour of her baby son. Mary's story continued to be played out in other royal palaces and castles, culminating with her execution, for treason by plotting against Elizabeth I, at the now ruined Fotheringay Castle in Northamptonshire on 8 February 1587.

It was at Holyroodhouse at the end of March 1603 that Mary's son, James VI of Scotland, heard that Elizabeth I had died and he had succeeded to the English throne. After that, he returned to Holyroodhouse only once, in 1617.

Bonnie Prince Charlie held a ball here in 1745 before his defeat at Culloden, and the flamboyant George IV visited Holyroodhouse in 1822, when Sir Walter Scott's romantic novels had made the whole of Britain Scotland-crazy. He attended a ball wearing the natty combination of full Highland dress and pink silk tights.

Today, Holyroodhouse is the official residence of the Queen when she visits Edinburgh each year, and she uses many of the State rooms which are open to the public at other times.

THE BANQUETING HALL at Brighton Pavilion during its heyday.

'A SQUARE BOX, a large Norfolk turnip and four onions' was the comment of William Cobbett, the author of *Rural Rides*, when he first saw Brighton Pavilion, and he was not alone in his criticism. Many of his contemporaries could not believe their eyes when they saw the extravagant minarets, and excitedly whispered about how much it had all cost.

Brighton Pavilion began life as a modest villa built by Henry Holland, commissioned by the eldest son of George III. The Prince originally asked for a Chinese interior. Yet when he became Prince Regent in 1811 he began to hanker for something more dashing and exciting, and commissioned John Nash, architect of Buckingham Palace and Regent's Park in London, to turn the pavilion into a suitably exotic and fantastic residence. Nash set to work, inspired by the Prince's love for all things oriental, and completed the building in 1822, two years after 'Prinny' had become George IV. After his experiences with Buckingham Palace, and the furore which its building had aroused, Nash must have had his answers off pat when questioned yet again about why the building was costing such a staggering amount of money. Questions were even asked in the House and rude cartoons of a grossly overweight and libidinous Prince Regent were published, with captions asking what hideous ideas he was going to come up with next. Today, these provide a salutary reminder that there is nothing new in criticizing royalty.

George IV died in 1830, and his successors were much less enthusiastic about the pavilion than he had been. His brother, William IV, was not interested in it and the next monarch, Queen Victoria, was frankly not amused. Her mind, which had narrowed under the prim influence of Prince Albert, must have boggled at the thought of what went on there when George IV was in residence, and in 1850 she was glad to sell the pavilion to Brighton. It languished, untenanted and empty, until after the Second World War when restoration work began. It is now a Mecca for lovers of oriental flights of fancy, and its architectural importance has finally been recognized.

THE HISTORY OF OXFORD is littered with royal events and experiences, some of which are distinctly happier than others. Queen Matilda, the last Norman sovereign in England (although she was never crowned) was imprisoned in Oxford Castle after her attempts to wrest the throne from Stephen ended in failure. On a snowy December night in 1142 Matilda, dressed in a white cloak, was lowered by rope down the castle walls and made her way across the frozen Thames to safety.

Matilda may have failed to rule England herself but her son, Henry II, succeeded to the throne in 1154 and began the Plantagenet dynasty. He also unwittingly began the first universities in England when he ordered that all English students at the continental universities should return home in 1167. This was to show his marked displeasure with the French for giving refuge to Thomas Becket, his defiant and troublesome Archbishop of Canterbury. The students all gathered around Oxford, although the first official university in Oxford (and Britain) was Merton College, founded in 1264.

Henry II built Beaumont Palace in Oxford and two of his sons, the future Richard I (Richard the Lionheart) and King John, were born there. The universities were growing all the time, often with royal patronage and sometimes with royal gifts. James I, who wrote what he considered to be great literary works (although he was the only one who thought so), gave a collection of these *oeuvres* to the Bodleian Library.

The college of Christ Church (see opposite) has several royal links, being founded by Cardinal Wolsey when he was still in favour. At that point it was called Cardinal College, but after Wolsey's death, Henry VIII founded the college all over again and gave it the new name of Christ Church. During the Civil War, after the Battle of Edge Hill in 1642, Charles I lived at Christ Church for three years and even set up a royal mint here. He finally fled the city in disguise. His son, Charles II, visited Oxford many times, and convened Parliament here in 1681 when there was an outbreak of plague in London.

In 1859 the beleaguered Edward, Prince of Wales, was sent up to study at Christ Church. However, his parents, Queen Victoria and Prince Albert, were worried about him falling in with the wrong company – an obsession with them that proved to be self-fulfilling – so arranged for him to lodge in a house by himself with a strict guardian to keep an eye on him. He was not even allowed to attend lectures with his fellow students in case they should prove unsuitable, and so the professors had to come to him. It is hardly surprising that the Prince wanted to rebel. His first opportunity came in 1861, when he was sent with the army to Ireland on manoeuvres. There, his fellow officers took pity on him and smuggled an actress into his tent for the night. Eventually, news of the escapade reached the Prince's parents who were horrified. When Prince Albert died in the same year, the distraught Queen Victoria was convinced that his early death had been hastened by shock over this incident, and declared that she would never again be able to look at 'that boy' without shuddering. She may not have gone that far, but relations were certainly always strained between them.

IN FEBRUARY 1970, Prince Charles returned to his old college, Trinity, to take part in a revue. He is shown here performing his monologue, 'Weather 'Tis Nobler', and blowing bubbles.

ALTHOUGH THE OLDEST COLLEGE in the city of Cambridge is Peterhouse, which was founded in 1284, it was to be another 150 years before any college had a royal founder. This was Henry VI, who laid the foundation stone for King's College in April 1441. Work was interrupted by the Wars of the Roses, when Henry was deposed and murdered, probably by his successor, the Yorkist Edward IV. In the meantime, however, Henry's wife, Margaret of Anjou, had founded her own college, Queen's College, in 1448, but it suffered badly when Henry lost the throne for the first time in 1461. The head of the college asked the new Queen, Elizabeth Woodville, to refound the college.

Margaret and Elizabeth were not the only female members of the royal family to favour Cambridge because the influential Margaret Beaufort, the mother of Henry VII, founded two colleges. The first was Christ's College, and the second was St John's, although the founding for this college took place posthumously in 1511, two years after her death. That was because her acquisitive grandson, Henry VIII, had tried to use the money she endowed to the college for himself. He apparently redeemed himself, however, not only releasing the money for Christ's College but founding another college himself. This was Trinity College, made up from three medieval establishments. In the 1960s, the present Prince of Wales was to study there.

Some notable diaries are housed in Magdalene College, and although the author was not royal he nevertheless was part of the Court at the time. He was Samuel Pepys, and Magdalene holds the diaries he kept from 1660-1669, at the beginning of the reign of Charles II. They detail two notable events of that decade – the Great Plague of 1665 and the Great Fire which swept through London the following summer.

FOR MANY PEOPLE, CIRENCESTER is synonymous with polo, for Cirencester Park is one of the three top polo clubs in England, along with Cowdray Park at Midhurst and Guards' at Smiths Lawn in Windsor Great Park. Each summer the grounds of all three clubs are thronged with spectators – and royal-watchers, for polo is the favourite game of Prince Charles.

The season at Cirencester starts each April, but does not begin until the end of the Badminton Horse Trials, and the Warwickshire Cup is played in late June every year. However, Cirencester is also interesting for people who are not polo *aficionados*, because the park itself is very beautiful and the town of Cirencester is interesting to explore and has many Roman connections.

Some people are bound to wander round the town with their eyes peeled for royal quarry, because Highgrove House, owned by Prince Charles, is not far away and there is always the chance that he may be glimpsed doing some shopping. When Princess Diana also lived at Highgrove House, shoppers at Cirencester and Tetbury (the nearest town to Highgrove) probably suffered from chronic neck pain, caused by constantly swivelling the head to and fro in the hopes of seeing *Her*.

Today, REGENT'S PARK is an orderly and elegant stretch of green space that lies between Camden Town and the top of Marylebone Road, but when Henry VIII's eager eye alighted on it in the 16th century the land belonged to the Abbess of Barking. Henry was not bothered by such a petty detail and converted the land into a royal hunting park. His daughter Elizabeth I hunted here, and Charles I allowed the park to be used as an artillery store during the Civil War. After the war, the park was sold with other Crown Estates, but it became Crown property again after the Restoration and was extensively farmed.

In the 1790s, with the end of the leases on the farms in sight, John Nash was commissioned to transform the 487 acres of land into something that would not only grace London but bring the Crown more money. His design was based on two strangely shaped circles, and he planned to scatter over fifty houses, each set in its own grounds, through the park. In the event, only eight were built. The Napoleonic Wars prevented work starting for several years, but Nash's patron, the Prince Regent, supported him through all the arguments and debates that raged about the new park and the terraces that would ring it.

In this century, another monarch made a valuable contribution to the park, when Queen Mary's Rose Garden was planted.

MEMBERS OF BRITISH ROYALTY have always been keen gardeners, so it is no surprise that they are closely linked with the development of the Royal Botanical Gardens, more commonly known as Kew Gardens. The town of Kew itself had been known to royalty since Tudor times, because of its proximity to the favoured Richmond Palace, but the gardens owe their existence to the Hanoverians.

George II and Queen Caroline started the trend in 1721 by buying a house, Richmond Lodge, in the Old Deer Park. The Queen laid out a garden but she was more interested in filling it with architectural follies than flowers. In 1728 she leased the Dutch House (now called Kew Palace) for 99 years and, although she was running a long-standing and bitter feud with her son, Frederick, Prince of Wales, he rented the White House which stood nearby and lived there with his family from 1731. After the Prince died in 1751 his widow, Augusta, Dowager Princess of Wales, continued to live at the White House until her death in 1771, at which point her son George III and his wife, Queen Charlotte, moved in. However, despite his father's improvements, the house was not big enough for the burgeoning royal family (there were 15 children) and they took over the Dutch House as well. The older children were taught 'practical gardening and architecture' in the grounds of the palace.

George ordered the demolition of the White House in 1802 and had another palace built in its place. This was a strange building, known as the Castellated Palace, which was never finished. By this time, George was becoming increasingly prostrated by the porphyria that would make his final years a misery. Queen Anne had probably suffered from the same disease, and George became plagued by bouts of insanity. Until 1810 these nightmarish episodes had only added up to six months of madness, but then he became permanently ill and his son, Prince George, was made the Prince Regent on 5 February 1811. The King, by now blind and in a world of his own, was packed off to a private set of rooms at Windsor Castle where he lived out the last sad years of his life. The only visible reminder that he was the King was the Star of the Order of the Garter, which he always wore pinned on his chest.

After his mother, Queen Charlotte, died in 1818 the Prince Regent ordered that the Dutch House should be pulled down, but then changed his mind. In any event, it was the end of the royal reign at Kew, and the Castellated Palace was demolished in 1827. The Dutch House, now known as Kew Palace, survives, but only the kitchen wing of the White House remains.

A common thread runs through the story of the Hanoverian monarchs – they all treated each other despicably. Years before he succeeded to the British throne George I divorced his wife, Sophia Dorothea, for adultery, then forbade her to see their children ever again and imprisoned her in the Castle of Ahlen in Germany for her rest of her life. Her lover, Count Konigsmark, vanished and popular rumour had it that George had ordered him to be hacked to pieces and then buried under the floor of his German palace. Later on, in England, George aroused public mockery with his choice of mistresses, one of whom was very tall (the 'Maypole') and the other very fat (the 'Elephant and Castle'). Naturally this alienated his son, George II, yet he appeared to have many of his father's traits, 'looking upon all men and women he saw as creatures he might kick or kiss for his diversion'. As Prince of Wales, he created a rival court which was much more lively and cultured than his father's. The two men had a very unhappy relationship and for a long time the only occasions on which they met were at the christenings of the Prince of Wales' children, but these always ended in dreadful rows.

Interestingly enough, as soon as George I died, George II rapidly became a carbon copy of his father. The gaiety of his Court fizzled out and was replaced by tedious evenings during which the new King relived his wartime memories at jaw-aching length. But the worst similarity between the two men was George II's relationship with his son, known as 'Poor Fred'. His father described him as 'the greatest ass, the greatest liar, the greatest canaille and the greatest beast in the whole world and we heartily wish he was out of it.' George cut his son's allowance to a quarter of what he himself had enjoyed when he was Prince of Wales, but despite all this (or perhaps because of it) 'Poor Fred' became popular. He was allowed to marry Princess Augusta of Saxe-Coburg-Gotha and the couple's combined popularity grew to such an extent that George II said it made him want to vomit.

Fred died in 1751 (George pretended to grieve but it was generally felt that he shed crocodile tears) and it was his son, George III, who succeeded to the throne when George II died in 1760. This new king was the first Hanoverian monarch to have been born and educated in England but the traditional problems between father and eldest son reasserted themselves. George III loved his son, the Prince of Wales (who later became George IV), but was far too protective of him and wanted to shield him from what the young Prince saw as the more exciting side of life. Naturally, by forbidding such pleasures the King merely made them seem more attractive than ever, and in December 1785 the Prince made a morganatic marriage to a widow, Mrs Maria Fitzherbert. This had been the only way to get her into bed, but although the couple loved each other the marriage presented too many insoluble difficulties to last long and in 1795 the Prince agreed to marry his cousin, Caroline of Brunswick, if Parliament would pay off his debts. The whole arrangement was a farce – when he met her, the Prince's first words were 'I am not well, pray get me a glass of brandy' and she found him a disappointment, too. They managed to produce a daughter, Princess Charlotte, after which the couple lived apart. Caroline was locked out of Westminster Abbey during George's lavish coronation and died shortly afterwards.

Years of hectic living had also taken their toll on the King, and George IV spent his last years at Windsor Castle, in considerable luxury, dreaming up new building projects and reminiscing about his role in the battle of Waterloo. As he had not been there no one knew if this was to annoy the Duke of Wellington (in which case he succeeded) or a sign that he was descending into madness like his father. One of the most colourful of all English monarchs, George IV died of internal bleeding on 26 June 1830.

The Hanoverians were the instigators of what we know today as Kew Gardens but they are not the only members of royalty who have stamped their personalities on the gardens. Many royal tea parties were held in the pretty Queen's Cottage, which was built for Queen Charlotte in 1771 and stands in the south-west corner of the Gardens. It is rather grand for a summerhouse, having two stories and a thatched roof, but its charm certainly appealed to Queen Victoria. She had given the Gardens themselves to the nation in 1841 and she gave the Queen's Cottage to the nation to celebrate her Diamond Jubliee.

The present garden (designed in 17th-century style) behind Kew Palace was opened to the public by Queen Elizabeth II in May 1969, and it is called the Queen's Garden. The Princess of Wales is also commemorated at Kew, in the futuristic glasshouse which was opened in 1987 and is named after her. Its ten different climates are controlled by computers.

PRINCESS ALEXANDRA and Sir Angus Ogilvy leave Thatched House Lodge for
the christening of their daughter Marina on 9 November 1966.

THIS IS ONE OF THE LOVELIEST STRETCHES of the London Thames, and it is not surprising that it has always attracted wealthy people. Today it is a large town especially popular with celebrities and actors, but until the early 16th century it was only a small hamlet, called Sheen, with a manor house. Even so, it had already attracted royal patronage.

Edward III enlarged the manor house and died there on 21 June 1377, no longer the great king who had galvanized England and proclaimed himself King of France. Instead, he was a pathetic old man in the sway of the barons he had tried to appease for so long. Even his mistress, Alice Perrers, apparently removed the rings from his fingers as he lay dying in the palace. The tyrannical Richard II succeeded to the throne, and he also enjoyed being at Sheen Palace – until his first wife, Anne of Bohemia, died there of plague in 1394. Distraught, Richard ordered that the palace should be demolished, although parts of it were left standing. Some of the dismantled palace was carted upriver to be used in the Tower of London, but Henry V had the palace repaired and royal patronage began again.

It was Henry VII who changed Sheen's fortunes. He liked the place so much that he made it one of his main royal residences, and even dug into his notoriously deep pockets to have it rebuilt after it was destroyed by fire in 1499. He wanted it to be a fitting tribute to the magnificence and might of the Tudors, whose dynasty had been founded by his father, and sure enough it was called 'this earthly and second paradise of our region of England'. He also changed its name to Richmond, after his earldom in Yorkshire. Henry's two sons, Arthur and Henry, were brought up here and Catherine of Aragon spent some time here during her period of widowhood when she was waiting for Henry to be old enough to be married to her. Henry VII died here in 1509, and in typical miserly fashion apparently left piles of gold hidden in lots of nooks and crannies in the palace. In 1540, after her divorce, Anne of Cleves was given Richmond Palace (where the news of the divorce had been broken to her) as part of her settlement and Henry used to visit her here. Perhaps because he had never been in love with her, Henry remained on good terms with her always, calling her his 'good sister'.

As the roll call of kings and queens continued, so did the royal use of Richmond Palace. Elizabeth I loved it here, calling it 'a warm winter box to shelter her old age', and died here on 24 March 1603. James I, however, had little interest in it although his son, Prince Charles, hunted here. Charles gave it to his bride, Henrietta Maria, as a wedding present and in due course it passed to their son, the future Charles II. However, Richmond Palace suffered a similar fate to many other royal residences when Charles I was executed in 1649, and it was broken up and partly destroyed. After the Restoration, when Charles II was safely on the throne again, he had the palace restored so his mother could live there, but it held too many unhappy memories for her and it passed to Charles' younger brother, James. When he became King, James asked Christopher Wren to rebuild the palace but the idea came to nothing and Richmond's great days were finally over. By the 18th century it was in a very sorry state, and today all that remains of this once glorious palace is the gateway on Richmond Green, which still bears the arms of Henry VII, and the Wardrobe.

Yet Richmond's role in royal lives still continues. There are two important royal houses – White Lodge and Thatched House Lodge – in Richmond Park. The park itself has royal connections – Charles I had it enclosed in 1637 to enlarge the grounds of Richmond Palace. Thatched House Lodge was built in about 1673 to house the ranger of the park, but in 1725 George II bought the rangership and gave it to the son of the then Prime Minister, Sir Robert Walpole. Today, Thatched House Lodge is lived in by Princess Alexandra and her husband, Sir Angus Ogilvy.

White Lodge was built by George II and was periodically lived in by his daughter, Princess Amelia. Incidentally, she adored hunting and was given the rangership of the park on the death of Walpole's son in 1751. White Lodge held miserable memories for Edward VII when he was Prince of Wales because his parents sent him to live here when he was sixteen. They said it would be good for him to have his own residence, but what they really wanted was to remove him from any undesirable influences at Court and London. Lack of psychological insight, especially on the prim Prince Albert's part, meant that the bored young Prince of Wales longed to start kicking up his heels in society. This he soon did, with a vengeance.

Princess May of Teck, who became Queen Mary, was born in White Lodge. She was originally engaged to the Prince of Wales' eldest son, Albert, Duke of Clarence, but he died unexpectedly in 1892 and in due course Princess May married his younger brother, George, instead. By all accounts she had a lucky escape because the Duke of Clarence had conducted a scandal-ridden life, and some authors have even suspected him of being Jack the Ripper.

Edward VIII was born at White Lodge on 23 June 1894, and in 1923 his brother and sister-in-law, the Duke and Duchess of York, spent their honeymoon here. It was originally intended that they should live here, but their busy lives made that impossible and they moved into a house in Piccadilly. In due course White Lodge was sold, but it has retained a royal connection – it is now the home of the Royal Ballet School.

THE INFANT PRINCE EDWARD, later Edward VIII, with his mother, who later became Queen Mary, and grandmother, the Duchess of Teck, in 1894. Both the Prince and his mother were born at White Lodge.

ONE OF THE GREAT SPLENDOURS of the Tudor age, Knole is a magnificent house, set in the midst of a huge deer park in the middle of Kent. It is linked with several kings, and indeed it would be odd if it had not been, because it is such a splendid place.

The original house was sold to Thomas Bourchier, Archbishop of Canterbury, in 1456, and the Archbishop lavished time and money on it before presenting it to the See of Canterbury in 1480. After his death, four other Archbishops lived here, but the last was the ill-fated Thomas Cranmer. Henry VIII knew Knole well, having visited it several times and even lodged his daughter, Princess Mary, there for six months in 1533. By 1538, he was determined to have it, and simply appropriated it from his Archbishop. However, like so many of the things that Henry coveted, once he owned Knole he lost interest in it. The business of acquiring objects and people seemed to please him much more than the enjoying of them. He spent money on the house but only visited it once, in 1541, when he broke his journey here. During the reign of Queen Mary Knole passed out of royal hands and into aristocratic ones, then passed back to the Crown on Mary's death. Queen Elizabeth I granted

it to her favourite, Robert Dudley, Earl of Leicester, in 1561 but when he returned it to her a few years later she immediately gave it to Thomas Sackville, her cousin. Knole had passed into the Sackville family and there it remained.

Successive members of the family served their respective monarchs at Court, and Lionel Sackville, the 7th Earl and 1st Duke of Dorset, was entrusted with the task of going to Hanover in 1714 to announce the death of Queen Anne to the new King, George I.

Knole's many connections with royalty are perhaps best celebrated by the King's Room – a truly fantastic room full of silver furniture and a French Louis XIV state bed covered with gold and silver brocade. This room is one of the most celebrated treasures of Knole, which is open to the public from spring to autumn each year. It is believed that the furniture came from Whitehall Palace, given to the 6th Earl of Dorset after the death of Mary II in 1694. The King's Room is a fitting testament to the grandeur of Knole – a house so large and sprawling that it has 7 courtyards, 52 staircases and 365 rooms. It is hardly surprising that Henry VIII's covetous eye should have been cast upon it.

SYON HOUSE has been the home of the Percy family, the Dukes of Northumberland, since 1594. It was built on the site of a Bridgettine monastery which had been founded by Henry V in 1415, but the monastery was taken over by Henry VIII in 1534 during his Dissolution of the Monasteries. He found a good use for it in the early 1540s, when it became the prison of his fifth wife, Catherine Howard, whom he had married secretly in July 1540 following his divorce from Anne of Cleves.

Catherine Howard was not as fortunate as her predecessor in her relationship with Henry, because he had her charged with adultery, after Archbishop Cranmer (who had successfully rid Henry of Catherine of Aragon and her successor, Anne Boleyn) had a quiet word in his ear in November 1541. Cranmer told Henry some interesting tales of Catherine's life before she met Henry, and of her various lovers, whom it was claimed included her cousin, Thomas Culpeper, and Francis Dereham, to whom she had been engaged. This in itself was bad enough at the time because it raised questions about the validity of her marriage to the King, but Catherine had continued to see both men after she was married to Henry – she must have enjoyed playing with fire, considering the combustible nature of her husband's temper – and these assignations were what led to her downfall and imprisonment at Syon House. At first, Henry believed these allegations were untrue, but changed his mind after Dereham and Culpeper confessed under torture. Both were beheaded in December 1541, yet for a while it seemed that a stay of execution had been served on Catherine, and Cranmer hoped to extricate the King from such an embarrassing marriage by claiming it was invalid – the same ploy that he had used with such success to free Henry of Catherine of Aragon. Such a move would have saved Henry's face (to some extent) and saved Catherine's neck, but Henry was furious, embarrassed and jealous, and wanted revenge. He never saw Catherine again, and she was sent off to Syon, with a reduced court. In the meantime, everyone around her was anxious to save their own skin at her expense, and the stories that were told about her behaviour as Queen soon left no one in any doubt that she was guilty of treason by adultery. Her death sentence had been unofficially passed.

In November 1541 Catherine was stripped of her title of Queen, and was indicted of promiscuity before her marriage and of adultery during it. Many of her servants and associates were sent to the Tower, having been declared guilty of 'misprison of treason' – of keeping quiet about Catherine's 'abominable, base, carnal, voluptuous and vicious life' before her marriage.

Catherine continued to live at Syon House, and various reports claimed that she was 'making good cheer'. This was in marked contrast to Henry, who was described as being 'little joyous'. Catherine, always unrealistic, still did not seem to be aware of her impending fate. It was only when she was taken from Syon House to the Tower on 10 February 1542 that she began to realize what would happen to her. She refused to board the barge that was waiting for her and had to be forced on to it by soldiers. As Catherine sailed along the Thames on her way to Traitor's Gate and the Tower of London, she saw the decapitated heads of her two lovers, Culpeper and Dereham, impaled on the spikes of London Bridge.

Recent executions at the Tower had been nothing short of butchery, and so the night before her execution Catherine asked to have the block sent to her room, so she could practise putting her head on it. The following day, on 13 February, as she stood on the scaffold at Tower Green, she is reputed to have said 'If I had married the man I loved instead of being dazzled with ambition all would have been well. I die a Queen but would rather have died the wife of Culpeper.' She was buried in the Tower's chapel of St Peter ad Vincula.

Syon House again provided the starting point for a journey to the Tower and its Green in 1553, when Henry VIII's sickly son by Jane Seymour, Edward VI, lay dying. This time the victim was Lady Jane Grey, a young girl who spent much of her life being the pawn of scheming, power-hungry men. She was the great grand-daughter of Henry VII and, as such, was a passport to power for whoever was wily enough to back her. Thomas, Lord Seymour, who married the widowed Catherine Parr after Henry VIII's death, had become Lady Jane's ward when she was nine, promising her parents that he would arrange her marriage to Edward VI. However, it was a plan over which he literally lost his head, being beheaded in 1549 for high treason. The next man to include Lady Jane in his ambitions was the Duke of Northumberland, the Lord Protector, who lived at Syon House. He was eager to retain his power over the throne, so arranged for his fourth son, Lord Guildford Dudley, to marry her, and then persuaded Edward VI to break his father's will and pass the crown to Lady Jane, cutting out his half-sister, Mary, completely. The marriage ceremony went ahead, but Lady Jane was miserable, disliking her in-laws and her husband.

Edward died on 6 July 1553 and the sixteen-year-old Lady Jane was told she had become Queen. She fainted on hearing the news, which was not generally made known until four days later. However, Mary had already heard of her brother's death, and many of the nobility rallied to her cause. The council which had passed Edward VI's new settlement in Lady Jane's favour revoked the document and Mary was proclaimed Queen on 19 July. Lady Jane was only too happy to renounce the throne. She had reigned for nine days.

Lady Jane and her father, the Duke of Suffolk, sailed up the Thames to the Tower, but her father obtained a pardon. Lady Jane and Lord Dudley were accused of high treason and sentenced to death. The execution was delayed but the involvement of the Duke of Suffolk in the Wyat rebellion sealed Lady Jane's fate. She and her husband were beheaded at the Tower on 12 February 1554, with Lord Dudley being executed in public on Tower Hill and Lady Jane being beheaded in private on Tower Green an hour later.

Keen gardeners, lepidopterists and fans of vintage cars are likely to visit Syon House for reasons that have little to do with poor Lady Jane Grey. That is because the grounds contain a very large garden centre, the London Butterfly House and the British Heritage Motor Museum. Syon House itself is also open to the public, who can marvel at the fantastic interiors which were designed by Robert Adam in the 1760s. The grounds were landscaped by Capability Brown, and were opened to the public in 1837. Among the rare trees and shrubs in the grounds are two mulberry trees which, it is claimed, were planted during the brief reign of Edward VI.

ONE OF THE GREAT Elizabethan architectural achievements, Burghley House was the home of Elizabeth I's chief minister and most trusted adviser, William Cecil. His career was chequered, because he worked closely with three successive monarchs, yet he managed to survive the vagaries of each of them. He served under the Dukes of Somerset and Northumberland, who acted as the Protectors of the young Edward VI, becoming Secretary of State in 1550 when the young King was still alive. When Mary I became Queen and reversed her father's Protestant reforms in the country, Cecil converted to Catholicism, but switched back again to Protestantism under Elizabeth I, who first appointed him Chief Secretary of State a fortnight after her accession and, in 1572, made him Lord High Treasurer, a post he held until his death in 1598. Among the tasks he carried out for Elizabeth was arranging the execution of Mary, Queen of Scots for treason in 1587. Elizabeth gave nicknames to all her advisers, and called Cecil her 'Spirit'.

Although he had his hands more than full looking after Elizabeth's concerns, which included preparing for the Spanish Armada and looking after his network of spies, he was apparently the principal architect of the house and supervised every stage of the building work. Cecil was created Lord Burghley in 1571 and is said to have refused an Earldom. However, after Cecil's death his son was created Earl of Exeter in 1605.

The Cecil family had bought the land after the monastery which had originally stood on it was dissolved by Elizabeth's father, Henry VIII, during his Dissolution of the Monasteries. The building was completed in 1589 although the interior was later altered considerably by John Cecil, the 5th Earl. Burghley was a house that appealed to royal taste, and when William III visited it during this period of redecoration he clearly had his eye on it, because he commented that it was 'too large for a mere subject'. However, such hints fell on stony ground because the house remained firmly in the hands of the Cecil family.

Today Burghley is still a feast for the eyes, not only from the outside with its wonderful architecture and grounds landscaped by Capability Brown, but also its magnificent interiors. Perhaps the most notable features of all are the painted ceilings and walls, most of which are the work of the 17th-century painter Antonio Verrio. Not surprisingly the work took him ten years, but his demands during that time were considered so outrageous by the 5th Earl (who had to import special Italian food for him) that his long-awaited departure was greeted with sighs of relief all round. Many of the paintings feature the gods of ancient Rome and Greece, and the painting in the 'heaven room' (the great saloon) is considered to be the masterpiece of Verrio's career. In fact, importing Italian food seems to be have been a very small price to pay for such a truly fantastic piece of art.

LOCAL LEGEND holds that a certain William Shakespeare poached the red and fallow deer that grazed in the grounds of Charlecote Park in Warwickshire in 1585. He was caught and prosecuted by Sir Thomas Lucy, the then owner of Charlecote Park and also local Justice of the Peace. Shakespeare retaliated by writing an uncomplimentary ballad about Sir Thomas. This caused an awful fuss and, to escape further punishment, Shakespeare fled from Stratford to London and started writing plays . . .

The house is a splendid monument to that great Elizabethan age which inspired Shakespeare's pen, although only the gatehouse is purely Elizabethan these days. The rest of the building was restored lovingly and lavishly by George and Elizabeth Lucy in the 1820s and 1850s. It seems only fitting that the river flowing behind the house should be the River Avon, which has so many associations with Shakespeare.

The house belonged to the Lucy family from the twelfth century onwards and only passed out of their hands in 1948. It is now owned by the National Trust. Although the house was visited by Elizabeth I, patron of William Shakespeare, the rooms are decorated in solid Victorian style, with no hint of the Elizabethan age.

Nearby is Edge Hill, where the first major battle of the Civil War took place in 1642.

Longleat was the first of the great Elizabethan country houses to be built, and work started in 1568. Sir John Thynne, newly released from the Tower of London, built the house to entertain Queen Elizabeth in suitably lavish style during her royal progresses each summer. The Queen was known for her frugal ways, and being entertained at her courtiers' expense for half of every year suited her reluctance to spend more money than she had to. However, it took 35 years before Elizabeth was able to stay here at Longleat because the first house burnt down as soon as it was completed.

In the 20th century, Longleat celebrated another landmark, when Lord Bath became the first peer of the realm to open his house to the public in 1949. The visitors flocked to see the magnificent house, yet Longleat still ate up money at an alarming rate, so in 1966 the Marquess of Bath hit on the revolutionary idea of turning part of the grounds into a safari park. It is interesting to speculate what Capability Brown, who originally landscaped the park, would have thought of such a scheme, but it has certainly become a very popular tourist attraction with its lions, tigers, giraffes, elephants, monkeys, wolves and gorillas, as well as many other animals.

THE STORY GOES that Princess Elizabeth was sitting under an oak tree in the grounds of the Old Palace at Hatfield in November 1558 when she heard that her half-sister Mary I had died and she had succeeded to the throne. She must have heard the news with mixed feelings – although her relationship with Mary had improved it had long been a difficult one. On the other hand, Elizabeth was now Queen. Today, the Old Palace is part of the larger Hatfield House. Hatfield House was built between 1607 and 1611 by Robert Cecil, son of the Queen's chief adviser, William Cecil, after Elizabeth's death. Until fifty years ago, the 15th-century brick palace was used as stables but it has now been restored to its former glory.

Old Palace was built by the Bishop of Ely in about 1497, but Elizabeth's father, Henry VIII, took it for himself after the Dissolution of the Monasteries, during which all Church lands passed to the Crown. Henry kept it as a residence for himself, and both his daughters, Mary and Elizabeth, stayed there. In fact, after his death and during the reign of Mary I, the Princess Elizabeth was a virtual prisoner here, so it is hardly surprising that she was an infrequent visitor once she became Queen.

Elizabeth could sense the xenophobic feeling in her kingdom following the death of the half-Spanish Mary and declared herself to be 'merely English'. This was exactly what her new subjects wanted to hear, and she began a reign which became a byword for powerful leadership and the flowering of the arts. Although her spinsterhood meant she lacked a direct heir, nevertheless she used her suitability as a wife as a diplomatic weapon, especially with France and Spain. Elizabeth had restored England to Protestantism, but the threat from the Catholic Mary Queen of Scots remained considerable. Mary was next in line to the throne, and was a constant thorn in Elizabeth's side because she had the backing of the French and the Spanish, and also of many of Elizabeth's own subjects. Finally, in 1586 Mary was implicated in a plot to assassinate Elizabeth and release Mary from her captivity. Although Elizabeth had at last found a reason for ridding herself of her cousin, she did not want the burden of Mary's death sentence on her conscience, so ordered that the order for her execution should be muddled up with various other official papers. That way, Elizabeth would sign it without realizing what it was. This she did, and then loudly blamed her secretary for not telling her what she had signed. But Mary's fate was sealed, nevertheless.

There is much to admire at Hatfield House, including the fantastic Marble Hall which runs for almost the full width of the house. The whole house is a monument to Jacobean architecture and design at its finest, and a life-size statue of James I, Elizabeth I's successor, stands guard above the mantelpiece in the King James Drawing Room. Yet, although Elizabeth died before Hatfield House was built, she is the monarch who is most closely associated with the house and whose ghostly presence seems to haunt it most. As well as two important and very beautiful portraits of her elsewhere in the house, there is also a piece of inventive (if not downright inspired) Elizabethan genealogy in the library – a parchment roll tracing Elizabeth's ancestors right back to Adam himself.

QUEEN VICTORIA presides over a gathering of her children and grandchildren in the grounds of Osborne House. Among the many members of the royal family shown here are a very young Prince Edward of York (later Edward VIII, third from the left and wearing a sailor suit), his mother the Duchess of York (seated on his left and holding his sister, Princess Mary) and his father the Duke of York (later George V), who is holding his brother (later George VI).

'OSBORNE IS REALLY TOO LOVELY. Charming, romantic and wild as Balmoral is – there is not that peaceful enjoyment that one has here of dear Osborne – the deep blue sea, myriads of brilliant flowers – the perfume of the orange-blossom, magnolias, honeysuckles, roses . . .' So wrote Queen Victoria to the Princess Royal in 1858. The Queen adored Osborne, because it was a house she and Prince Albert had been able to buy and renovate between them.

When she succeeded to the throne in 1837 the Queen inherited three royal residences – Buckingham Palace, Windsor Castle and Brighton Pavilion. She was very dubious about Brighton because she disliked its associations with the rackety Prince Regent and the other two buildings were so formal that she longed to have a retreat of her own where she could relax and escape from the rigours of attending to affairs of State. Osborne House on the Isle of Wight was just what she wanted, especially as it had a private beach and a lovely view of the Solent. It also had about 1000 acres of land which Prince Albert set about landscaping – his attempts to alter the grounds of Buckingham Palace and Windsor Castle had been frowned upon by the Department of Woods and Forest.

However, the original Osborne House only had sixteen bedrooms and was therefore too small for Queen Victoria's vast family and retinue, and Thomas Cubitt was commissioned to rebuild the house from Prince Albert's designs. The new Osborne House would consist of two buildings – the Pavilion Block for the royal family and the Main Block for the household – and would be built in Italianate style. Prince Albert planted many trees in the grounds, to ensure as much privacy for his family as possible, and a tiny chalet, known as the Swiss Cottage, was shipped from Switzerland in sections and erected in the grounds in 1853. The royal children gardened, learnt to cook and even entertained their parents to tea here. Another chalet was built nine years later to house the children's collections.

After the untimely death of Prince Albert in 1861, the bereft Queen Victoria swiftly came to Osborne to find solace in the surroundings in which her husband had been happiest. She herself died here in the evening of 22 January 1901, in her bedroom, after a short illness. Her body was laid in state in the dining room before being buried at Frogmore, Windsor.

Edward VII had no interest in maintaining Osborne, and gave it to the nation. During his mother's lifetime he had refused to visit the place. After his mother's death, he had a highly satisfying time smashing many of the memorials that she had erected to her beloved Scottish servant, John Brown. This man had been something of an embarrassment to the family in the 1880s. In smart London circles, she was even referred to as 'Mrs Brown', because popular gossip held that she had married John Brown in a secret ceremony.

At first the State apartments were opened to the public and Queen Victoria's suite was kept private, but the present Queen opened these to the public in 1954.

Above GEORGE, PRINCE OF WALES, later King George V, with his son Prince Henry (Duke of Gloucester), Sandringham, 1902.
Far right GEORGE VI inspecting the harvest at Sandringham with the royal family in 1943.

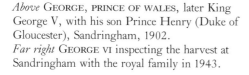

SANDRINGHAM was bought by Queen Victoria in 1861, when the future Edward VII, then Prince of Wales, came of age. But the original house swiftly became too small and was rebuilt in Jacobean style in 1870. The architect chosen, A J Humbert, was dear to Queen Victoria's heart as he had designed the late Prince Albert's Mausoleum at Windsor, but Edward VII had other ideas and developed the estate into one of the best game reserves in the country.

'The place I love better than anywhere else in the world', is how George V described Sandringham, and he spent much of his father's reign, from 1892 to 1910, here. He would shoot by day and work on his beloved stamp collection in the evenings. He died here on 20 January 1936 and one of the traditions that died with him was 'Sandringham time'. Edward VII, impatient to have as much shooting as possible, had ordered that all Sandringham clocks be set half an hour fast, and that was the way they had remained. It was one of the traditions that George V loved about the place. Yet the night he died, the new king, Edward VIII, ordered that all the clocks be changed back to Greenwich Mean Time.

That same year, Edward VIII, who was obsessed with making ends meet despite having a very handsome income, asked his brother Bertie (later George VI) to see how the running costs of Sandringham, a place he adored, could be reduced – hardly tactful considering the

lavish amounts of money that were being spent by the King on a certain Mrs Simpson's happiness and creature comforts. When he abdicated in December 1936, Edward VIII 'sold' Balmoral and Sandringham to his brother – although his father had left him these houses in his will, they had been given to him as the king and not to him personally. George VI was no doubt happy to take part in the transaction, as he regarded Sandringham as home, and died here on 6 February 1952 after spending an enjoyable day shooting hare.

It was Queen Victoria who had begun the family round of holidays, with Christmas always spent at Sandringham, Easter at Windsor and August and September at Balmoral in Scotland, but her great-great-granddaughter, the present Queen, was forced to change that tradition in the 1960s, when the family grew too large for a Sandringham Christmas and they had to go to Windsor instead.

Until 1966, when the royal Christmas was spent at Windsor, the family would travel from London to Sandringham by train, arriving at nearby Wolferton station. The station was always kept in shining readiness for a royal visit and although the line has since been taken up, the station survives as a tiny museum which can be visited. Sandringham can also be visited each summer. You can even drink the fruits of Sandringham if you wish – many acres of land are devoted to blackcurrant growing, with the annual harvest sold to the company who make Ribena.

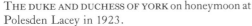
THE DUKE AND DUCHESS OF YORK on honeymoon at
Polesden Lacey in 1923.

IN THE 1920S AND 1930S, the Regency villa of Polesden Lacey, on the edge of Box Hill, was a glittering Mecca for many members of British society. It was a time when society hostesses presided over dinner tables full of the great, the good and the occasionally notorious, and Mrs Ronnie Greville of Polesden Lacey was one of the most assiduous and eager hostesses of all. In 1891 she married the Hon. Ronald Greville, a man with wonderful connections. He was a close friend of George Keppel, whose wife, Alice, was the mistress of the Prince of Wales, and Mrs Greville began climbing her way to the top of the social ladder. She and her husband bought Polesden Lacey in 1906, by which time the Prince of Wales had become King Edward VII.

By April 1923 her success was assured, because the newly married Duke of York and his young bride, Lady Elizabeth Bowes-Lyon, spent a few days of their honeymoon at Polesden Lacey. It seemed that anyone who was anyone gravitated to Polesden Lacey at some time or another, drawn there not only by the infinite luxury but also the interesting company, and the thrill of meeting members of both British and European royalty. Even Mrs Greville's butler and footman, both of whom were usually drunk, could not keep her guests away. Once, when the butler was even more incapable than usual while serving dinner, Mrs Greville scribbled a note which said 'You are drunk. Kindly leave the room' and handed it to him. He read it, laid it on the plate of one of her guests who thought it was for him, and tottered away.

By the 1930s, the social climate was changing in more ways than one. Most of the society hostesses loved the idea that politics was being discussed in their drawing and dining rooms by the very men who created it, and Mrs Greville was no exception. Rumours of another war with Germany were gathering momentum and society opinion was dividing into pro-Germany and anti-Germany factions. Mrs Greville was pro-German in the pre-war years, much to the annoyance of Winston Churchill and Harold Nicolson.

But there was another schism growing in the ranks of English society, and it concerned the Prince of Wales. He loved society and was a great favourite of Mrs Greville. Yet in the mid-1930s his growing friendship with Mrs Simpson, a twice-married American woman who was widely believed to be his mistress, was causing alarm. Many people, including the Duchess of York (later Queen Elizabeth), did not warm to Mrs Simpson, who appeared to dominate the Prince to such an extent that people wondered which of them was royal. But to the Prince, Mrs Simpson was the only woman he would ever love, and he adored everything about her from her pencil-thin figure to the way she bullied him.

By 1936, when George V died and, to his horror, the Prince of Wales became Edward VIII, society opinion really began to be affected. The King was obviously determined to stay with Mrs Simpson at all costs, and began to appear in public with her in a way that left few people in doubt about the true nature of their relationship. He was hardly the first king to have had a mistress, but that was not the problem. In fact, the problem was fourfold – Mrs Simpson was a commoner and she was American. By the autumn of 1936 she was in the throes of divorcing her second husband; and the King was talking of a morganatic marriage.

Stanley Baldwin, who was then the Prime Minister, the Archbishop of Canterbury and Geoffrey Dawson, the highly influential editor of *The Times*, were united in their opposition to the marriage, which would mean that the King remained royal while his wife remained a commoner, and any children would have no claim to the throne. It was the course taken by George IV when he secretly married Mrs Fitzherbert in 1785 and was one pursued quite often in European royal families, but it was unthinkable in 1930s Britain, and on 2 December 1936 Baldwin told the King that the Cabinet had rejected the idea. This left the King with three choices: to go against his Government and marry Mrs Simpson in time for his coronation in May 1937 – in which case they would all resign; to leave Mrs Simpson – which he would never do; or abdicate. Matters moved ahead with frightening speed for the Duke and Duchess of York, who found themselves facing the staggering prospect of the throne. Edward VIII abdicated on 10 December 1936. As the newly created Duke of Windsor, he left England the same night for his ultimate destination of Vienna, where he would wait out the months until Mrs Simpson's divorce became final and they could marry.

The Duke and Duchess of York, now King George VI and Queen Elizabeth, may have been shattered by the events but many people inside the royal circle and in the Government were immensely relieved. There had been grave doubts about not only Mrs Simpson and the King's fitness to rule, but national security as well. Mrs Simpson had dined at the German Embassy in 1935 and there were rumours and suspicions about her political sympathies.

After the war, these rumours finally burst forth in a riot of fact, suspicion, conjecture, spite and malice. Mrs Simpson had been spying for the Germans, spying for the Italians, had been a prostitute in China, the Duke and Duchess of Windsor had been planning with the Germans to head a republican Britain after Germany had won the war . . . These rumours continue even today, over fifty years since the drama was played out. It is one of the great stories of the twentieth century.

THE TABLOID PRESS HAS HAD SEVERAL field days over the activities that are supposed to have taken place at Highgrove House in recent years, during the marriage of the Prince and Princess of Wales. So much so, in fact, that the house itself – which is a most elegant Georgian building in the classical style – has been completely neglected in the blizzard of supposition and sheer invention about what has gone on within its stone walls. So rather than dwell any further on bugged telephone conversations and leaps down long flights of stairs, let us consider the house and garden instead.

Prince Charles bought Highgrove in 1981, the year of his marriage to Lady Diana Spencer. As well as providing him with his first home away from the rest of the royal family, it has given him ample scope to practise and refine his considerable gardening and farming skills. The Prince is well known (and, in some quarters, virtually reviled) for his love of

gardens, plants and ecology, yet in the first two interests at least he is following in the family footsteps. Most members of the royal family through the centuries have been keen gardeners, with some monarchs playing pivotal roles in the history of British gardens. William III and Mary II, for example, were responsible for much of the garden structure at Hampton Court, and Augusta, Princess of Wales, who was the mother of George III, played a vital part in the development of Kew Gardens.

Even Highgrove itself has strong associations with an important garden, although there was little garden of any consequence when the Prince bought the land in 1981. At the end of the 19th century, Highgrove belonged to one Colonel Mitchell, a man whose name may have been forgotten by many but whose creation, Westonbirt Arboretum, is renowned throughout the world.

TODAY GOODWOOD is known not only for its wonderful mansion, Goodwood House (see left), but also for the racetrack (see opposite, far right), and both have strong royal connections. In fact, the present Queen is such a keen racegoer that, while staying at the house for the July races, she has held Privy Council meetings here.

Originally, Goodwood House was a hunting lodge, and was bought in 1697 by the 1st Duke of Richmond. He was the illegitimate son of Charles II but this was hardly a matter for comment because all Charles II's fourteen children were illegitimate. The 1st Duke of Richmond's mother was Louise de Kéroualle (popularly believed to be a French spy), but other notable mistresses of the 'Merry Monarch', as Charles II was called, included the Duchess of Portsmouth and, most famously of all, Nell Gwynne.

It was the 3rd Duke who extended the original hunting lodge into Goodwood House as we know it today, and also laid out the racecourse. He was British Ambassador at Versailles and in the course of his travels amassed some priceless treasures. Goodwood House is full of them, as many other intriguing artefacts were left behind by visiting royalty when they stayed at the house for the racing at 'Glorious Goodwood'. They include Queen Victoria's Fabergé walking stick, bullets fired at Waterloo and many important paintings.

GEORGE V photographed in the royal box at Goodwood in July 1927. The man standing behind him is his private secretary, Lord Stamfordham.

Anyone who believes firmly that Things Aren't What They Were need look no further than Royal Ascot, which is one of the highlights of the English social season. For a week in June (usually blighted by heavy rain throughout) racegoers, gamblers, socialites, the royal family and dedicated royal-watchers make their way to Berkshire and the Ascot racecourse. It was not all that long ago that divorced people were not allowed inside the Royal Enclosure, presumably because their very presence would be guaranteed to make the royal flesh creep. All that changed, however, when Queen Mary withdrew her veto. As it turned out, that is just as well, otherwise such members of the royal family as Princess Margaret and Princess Anne would not be allowed inside their own enclosure.

For most people who attend Ascot religiously each June their presence has little or nothing to do with racing. The horses rank a very poor second to the spectators and those famous Ascot hats which really come into their own each Ladies Day.

It is interesting to speculate on what Queen Anne would have thought of it all. She ordered that the racecourse should be built, in 1711, but as she is not renowned in history for her sense of humour, nor her sense of fun, it is unlikely that she would be impressed by Ascot today.

Race-going appeals greatly to some members of the present royal family, and the Queen and the Queen Mother are both owners of race horses themselves, as well as being avid and expert assessors of bloodstock.

In June 1954 the Queen Mother and Princess Margaret arrived together in an open coach for the first day of that year's Royal Ascot meeting.

In June 1932, Ascot was attended by King George V and Queen Mary, who shielded herself from the sun with a large umbrella held aloft so as not to obscure her face from the watching crowds.

ᴇᴀᴄʜ ᴊᴜʟʏ ᴛʜᴇ ᴘʀᴇᴛᴛʏ ᴛᴏᴡɴ of Henley-on-Thames becomes a Mecca for boating enthusiasts as the Royal Henley Regatta gets underway. This annual event began in 1839 but was not given its royal status until Prince Albert became its patron in 1851. Although the regatta was designed for amateur rowers, participants had to come from the correct social class and anyone 'engaged in a menial duty' was excluded from taking part. This led to some unhappy decisions, such as the banning of a crew of First World War servicemen in 1919 who wanted to take part in a peace regatta. It was a decision that made King George V furious.

Other royal visits to Henley have been more happy. Prince William of Orange stopped here in 1688, on his way from the Netherlands to London and the English throne, to meet a deputation from the House of Lords. He was assured that public support for him was growing all the time, and he continued with his army into London to assume the throne which his father-in-law, James II, had so hurriedly vacated.

A CONVALESCENT GEORGE V is pushed around the grounds of Craigwell House, where he stayed with Queen Mary in 1929. Their young grand-daughter, Princess Elizabeth, joined them in March.

I F SIR RICHARD HOTHAM, the founder of the seaside resort of Bognor, had had his way the town would have been called 'Hothampton'. Sir Richard was a rich London hatter of the late 18th century, and he hoped to lure fashionable society away from nearby Brighton to his new resort. He built Dome House to encourage tourists, and was rewarded when the first royal visitor arrived for a series of visits – Princess Charlotte, only daughter of George IV. It was her father, of course, when he was Prince Regent, who had done so much to establish Brighton's reputation. Now his daughter gave Bognor a quiet respectability which was a world away from the racy, rather insalubrious atmosphere of Brighton at the time.

Queen Victoria called the town her 'dear little Bognor' but it earned its final stamp of approval, and its second name of 'Regis', when George V came here in 1929 to convalesce after a near-fatal bout of bronchial pneumonia, complicated by blood poisoning and a weakened heart. The King stayed at a secluded manor house at Aldwick, to the west of the town, and although the bracing sea air and the enforced rest were taken on the orders of his doctors, he added another important factor – the company of his favourite grandchild, Princess Elizabeth. A large sandpit was dug in a corner of the garden for her and she duly arrived in March 1929. Queen Mary often joined her grand-daughter in the sandpit to make sandcastles and when the King appeared on the sea front Princess Elizabeth was at his side and waved excitedly at the crowds. They all cheered.

A ROYAL COMMAND CONCERT held at the Royal Albert Hall on 24 May 1935 was attended by
George V and Queen Mary in the royal box.

IT WAS PRINCE ALBERT who first had the idea of building a network of museums, colleges
and a large hall in South Kensington. He wanted to use the profits from the Great
Exhibition, but the scheme failed to get off the ground when he first suggested it in 1851 and it
was not until after his death ten years later that things finally started to happen. Sir George
Gilbert Scott was chosen to design an exhibition hall, plus a memorial for the late Consort, and
funds were raised by selling 999-year leases on over 1300 of the seats at £100 each. The hall
was opened in 1870 by the Prince of Wales, because his mother's overwhelming emotion
meant she could not bring herself to attend the ceremony.

The hall was duly opened – and immediately a most embarrassing problem arose. The
acoustics were so strange in the hall that the closing 'Amen' of the prayers reverberated around
the building. Perhaps it is just as well that Queen Victoria was not there as she might have
thought it was the shade of her beloved Albert trying to make contact with her. If so, he was
remarkably fond of the eponymous hall because every event that took place there was marred
by the echo. Sir Thomas Beecham once said that the hall was suitable for all sorts of things but
music wasn't one of them.

Despite the echo, the hall continued to be used for concerts and charity balls. Boxing was
another activity that took place in the hall and in 1941 the annual Promenade Concerts,
brainchildren of Sir Henry Wood, moved here from the Queen's Hall after it was bombed.
In 1968 money from a government grant was used to try to correct the echo, and strange
saucer-like objects were suspended from the roof. Today the hall is still home to the Proms
each summer, as well as many other concerts (ranging from classical to rock music),
ceremonies and charity events. Queen Victoria would be very proud.

THE V & A, as the Victoria and Albert Museum is popularly known, was developed with the active encouragement of Prince Albert and with the objective of continuing the aims of the Great Exhibition of 1851, which had been to promote the arts and sciences.

Prince Albert had organized the Great Exhibition, which was visited by over six million people, and wanted to continue his work. It increased his national popularity, which did not run very high at the time, and helped him to look as if he were a useful member of the royal family. He was Queen Victoria's greatest adviser in private, but his talents were not widely recognized in public.

In 1857 the Museum of Ornamental Art and the School of Design were both moved from their original premises to South Kensington, where over 80 acres of land had been bought with the profits from the Great Exhibition. This vast tract of land was to be the site of a whole network of museums, schools, colleges and concert halls, all of which were built in due course and which still stand today, and include the Royal Albert Hall, the Science Museum, the Natural History Museum, Imperial College and the Victoria and Albert Museum.

The School of Design was installed in a series of wooden sheds, while the Museum of Ornamental Art was given a peculiar construction, made from corrugated sheet iron, cast iron and glass, and painted with green and white stripes to stop it frightening the horses. Queen Victoria opened this monstrosity on 22 June 1857 and its first director was Sir Henry Cole – one of the men, incidentally, who is credited with inventing the Christmas card.

As the years wore on the corrugated iron building and the wooden sheds became crammed with national and international treasures – and swiftly turned from crammed to cramped. Prince Albert had died in 1861 from typhoid and, robbed of his considerable inflence, the Museum had to struggle on in its uncomfortable premises until it was finally accepted that one huge building would have to be created to contain the priceless collection that had been amassed. So, in 1890, it was announced that there would be a competition for the best design of a new building. Eight architects entered and Aston Webb won, although it was another nine years before the foundation stone was laid. This important ceremony was performed on 17 May 1899 by Queen Victoria, who also decreed that the museum should be given its present name. This was one of the Queen's last public engagements.

The museum cost over £600,000 to build and was officially opened by King Edward VII, on 26 June 1909. The central tower, which is shaped at the top like a crown, makes the V & A instantly recognizable, as do the statues of Queen Victoria and Prince Albert, which stand above the main entrance and are flanked by statues of King Edward VII and Queen Alexandra.

The museum is one of the great success stories of the Victorian age, and is still thriving today. Controversies flare up from time to time about the policies of the directors and trustees, but there is no mistaking the outstanding contribution that the Victoria and Albert Museum makes to Britain's cultural heritage and appreciation of fine art.

INDEX

GEORGE VI AND QUEEN ELIZABETH with Princess Elizabeth and Princess Margaret in the grounds of Royal Lodge in July 1946.

ACKNOWLEDGEMENTS

Tim Kendall and Jason Hawkes wish to acknowledge the help of Mark Barry-Jackson of Aeromega Helicopters.

The photographs in this book were all taken by Jason Hawkes with the exception of the following:

Aerofilms: 29, 30, 36, 37, 42, 53, 61, 63, 64, 65, 96, 97, 109, 133, 136 (top); Edinburgh Photographic Library/Peter Davenport: 17, 34, 99, 101; Mary Evans Picture Library: 12, 28, 32, 47, 70, 88, 98, 139 (top left); Angelo Hornak: 62; Hulton Deutsch Collection Limited: 1, 14 (bottom right), 21, 22, 35, 39 (left), 40, 52, 55, 56, 73, 74, 77, 78 (top right), 81, 85 (bottom), 87, 92, 103, 107 (right), 114, 115 (left), 129, 130 (left and right), 135 (left), 136 (bottom left and right), 140; National Trust Photo Library: 132; Popperfoto: 79 (left); Rex Features: 43; Skyscan Balloon Photography: 14 (top), 15, 72, 128; Adam Woolfitt/Robert Harding Picture Library: 108, 137.